Reading this book is in its
hand of God. This teaching will deliver you from fear and open the door for God's plan for your life.

—John Dawson, Founder
International Reconciliation Coalition

This book provides clear and compelling insight for those who wonder what a life of submission to God should be like. Written with a generous use of Scripture and a well-balanced portion of personal experiences and anecdotes, it is a must-read for all who seek a life of significance.

—James Ryle
President, Truth *Works* Ministries

I love books that are packed with Scripture, and *The Mighty Hand of God* is just that. And I love books that deliver practical truths right to my front door where I can use them. This one delivers. Dale Evrist will help you find your place under God's strong hand where you will be encouraged, challenged and drawn into a deeper relationship with our Lord Jesus Christ.

—Ron Mehl, senior pastor
Beaverton Foursquare Church
Beaverton, Oregon

It is abundantly clear that Dale Evrist has graphically experienced "the mighty hand of God," which is nowhere more clearly explained than here. Addressing this subject is long overdue, but in reading this I know it is right on time.

—Wayne Cordeiro, Senior Pastor
New Hope Christian Fellowship O'ahu
Honolulu, Hawaii

This book will change the way you live by reteaching you the meaning of true humility. With practical and powerful suggestions, Dale Evrist leads us back to the most exciting and fulfilling place we live: under the mighty hand of God.

—Daniel A. Brown, Ph.D.
The Coastlands
Aptos Foursqure Church

At last, a thoroughly modern take on surrender and submission. Dale Evrist smooths the path for much success in our families, our businesses and our churches. This is a must-read for a generation in search of integrity.

—Ralph Moore, Senior Pastor
Hope Chapel
Kaneohe, Hawaii

The Mighty Hand of God is a book about God—who He is, what He is like, His desires and intentions. But it is also a book about us—how through truly placing our lives under His mighty hand we can overcome the fears, doubts and other obstacles that prevent us from experiencing His best.

—Steve Overman, Senior Pastor
Faith Center
Eugene, Oregon

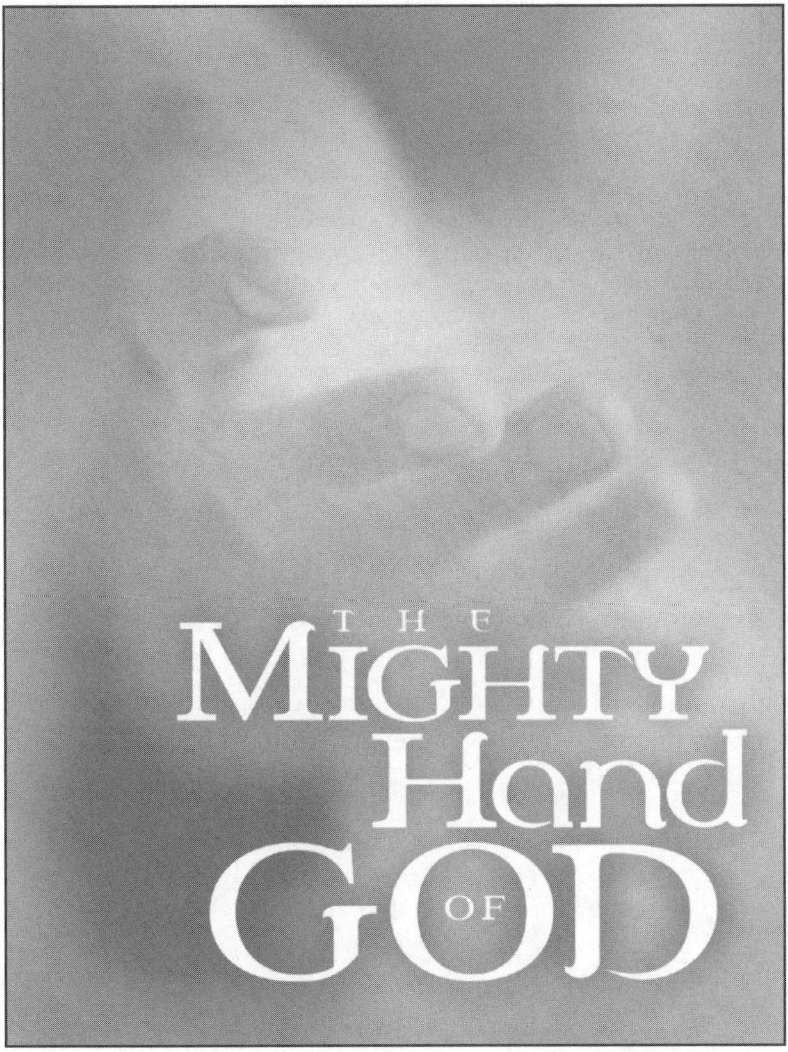
THE
MIGHTY
Hand
OF
GOD

DALE EVRIST

Charisma
HOUSE
A STRANG COMPANY

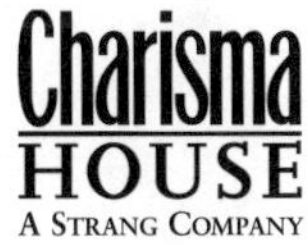

The Mighty Hand of God by Dale Evrist
Published by Charisma House
A Strang Company
600 Rinehart Road
Lake Mary, Florida 32746
www.charismahouse.com

Library of Congress Catalog Card Number: 00-102302
International Standard Book Number: 0-88419-658-5

04 05 06 07 08 — 7 6 5 4 3 2
Printed in the United States of America

To the memory, ministry and mentorship of
Roy Hicks, Jr., who modeled living by
prophetic assignment under the mighty hand of
God as well as any man I have ever known.

ACKNOWLEDGMENTS

I would like to express my love, thanks and deep appreciation to:

- My wife, Joan, my partner in life and ministry who has lived the message of this book and has helped me stay committed to strive always to live by "prophetic assignment."
- My children, Janelle and Joel, who have made me very proud by their own commitment to bring their lives under God's mighty hand, and for their sacrifice and generosity in sharing their dad's time with others.
- My dad and mom, for raising me in an atmosphere of strong faith and showing me that God's hand was able to accomplish the impossible.
- Dad and Mom Romano, for raising a great lady to be my wife and for treating your son-in-law as your own flesh and blood.
- Pastor Jack Hayford, for leading me to Christ when I was a teenager, and for all of the modeling and mentoring of faith, obedience and integrity since that time.
- Brian Glassford, my "Jonathan," without whose help I could not have completed this project.
- Lisa Glassford, my assistant, for all of your hard work, expecially in the formative stages of gathering materials for the book.
- The New Song staff, for their help and encouragement throughout the process of birthing my first book.
- Pastor Chuck and Dortha Elam, Susan Shipsey, Ashley Hagan and all of those intercessors who faithfully prayed me through the process.
- The New Song family, for being a community of faith and enabling the message of this book to became names, faces and lives rather than simply theory.
- My Foursquare family and leadership, Dr. Risser, Jerrod Roth and especially Glenn Burris, Jr., for adopting me into our movement and being incredible servant-leaders and friends.
- Lastly, to the incredible team at Creation House: Steve, Joy, Rick, Jimmy, Barb, Carol, Daphne, Mike, Jay and others, for believing in this "rookie writer" and working so hard to get this message out.

Contents

Foreword

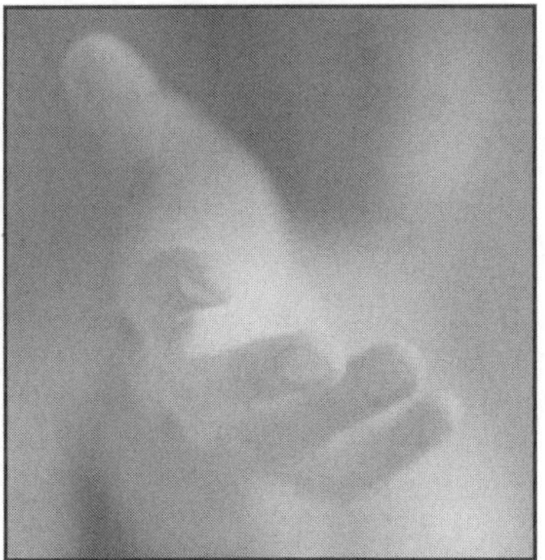

We are living in both the best and the worst times of the church of our Lord Jesus Christ.

Unquestionably, the best things in all church history are happening in yours and my lifetime. I hesitate to begin enumerating them, because I have only been asked to write a foreword to my friend's—indeed, a son's—book. This, when only a book would suffice, for the Spirit's outpouring across the face of the earth is recording marvels of remarkable miracles, of unprecedented church growth, of nations being shaken by God, of multitudes being saved as glory is revealed in so many ways.

But there is a downside to this. Amid blessings it seems "presumption" too often abounds. By "presumption," I refer to that attitude born of confusion that either tolerates shabby living in the name of grace or flaunts the habits of unsubmission or unaccountability among spiritual leaders, simply because "he (or she) seems so anointed and gifted." The inevitable is that very bad times will be forthcoming—when "humbling oneself under the mighty hand of God" is deemed unnecessary or optional.

That gets us to the nub of the subject that opens this book, and it also tells us something about the character of the author.

People don't write about subjects like this unless they are committed to living it. Dale Evrist is that—a committed shepherd, gifted, anointed and prospering spiritually in his ministry, but who is determined to let none of those blessings turn his eyes from the price of leadership: humility and submission.

He is not arrogant about it. He isn't pushy or legalistic in approaching the call to this dimension of discipleship. Nor is he unwilling to share some of his own lessons learned and steps of stumbling—for none of us are without our failures as we pursue Jesus' course—Submission 101 (which, by the way, is renewed as a course for all of us *every year of our lives).*

Dale is a good guy. He is a faithful husband, a loving dad, a servant-hearted pastor, a visionary leader, a devoted worshiper (and songwriter), a responsive friend and . . . a budding author. I think you will like meeting him here.

And I am sure you will profit from the solid, refreshing and worthwhile way he opens God's Word to point in practical ways to *The Way—Jesus.* He's the One who makes the best of times to keep on being that, and who, in the midst of the worst of times, can work His redemptive solutions and bring us through and out!

He's the One whose mighty hand reaches to save, and the One who calls us to live under that hand, to learn that always, eventually, the way of the cross is the true way of the winner.

—Jack W. Hayford
Founding Pastor, The Church On The Way
Chancellor, The King's College & Seminary
Van Nuys, California

Lay It Down

Lay it down
Lay it down.
Lay your dreams and visions down
Underneath His mighty hand;
Lay it down.
He will take your earthly treasure
And then offer heaven's crown,
When you make the choice by faith
To lay it down.

—Lyrics by Dale Evrist

Chapter 1

Do You Need a Hand?

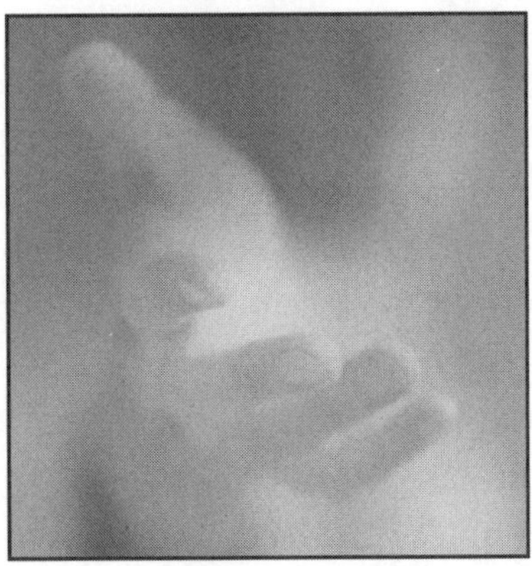

Just as a small child reaches to grasp his father's hand as he walks along a path he's never traveled before, God invites you to grasp His hand as He leads you into the purpose, destiny and future He has prepared for your life. God never intended for you to walk your life's path by following your own plans and purposes. He doesn't want you trudging through dark alleys and up mountains alone. He has a master plan for you—one that will guide you into a far greater destiny that you have hoped for or dreamed of without Him. He wants you to live by this master plan—one He designed for you even before He created our earth.

My greatest desire—and probably yours—is to live a life that works! God wants you to know that your life can work—it is supposed to work! But it isn't education, background, advantage and opportunity that make it work. It is taking the mighty hand of God that makes it work.

Do you need a hand? God's mighty hand of favor and blessing is extended toward you. I'm sure you have heard the expression, "Talk to the hand." Here's a new one: "Get under the Hand!"

God has an incredible future for you—but you're going to need to get under His hand. That hand is a hand of *promotion, provision, protection, power* and *purpose.* And when He supports us with His mighty hand, it opens the door for dynamic blessings to come into our lives. They are all redemptive, life-giving attributes that He adds to the person who submits himself or herself under His mighty hand.

These attributes affect our lives in these specific ways:

Promotion—God's mighty hand lifts us up to greater levels of influence and fruitfulness in serving the body of Christ and in the world. Perhaps as a child your father or mother took a firm hold on your hand, led you into a room of adults and proudly stated, "This is my child, and I am so proud of him (or her). I just wanted you to meet him." Perhaps he or she went on to list your achievements and skills. God does this, too. He tells the world, "This is My child, and I am so proud of him." He leads you into opportunities and blessings you could never find without placing your hand in His hand of direction. He's your heavenly Father—and He sees you and your future through the eyes of a loving parent who wants you to succeed in all you do. God's mighty hand promotes you to a life impossible without Him.

Provision—God provides us with everything we need physically, emotionally, relationally, spiritually and financially. Through His mighty hand of provision we find abundant life. Under His hand we are carefully led into green pastures, past fresh mountain streams of blessing. His hand of provision prepares a table of blessing in full view of our enemies. With that hand grasping ours we "shall not want." (See Psalm 23.)

Protection—Did your father ever grasp your shoulder with his hand and pull you out of the path of danger? Did your mother ever raise her hand to say, "No, you can't go there...you can't do that—it's too dangerous for you"? As we walk hand in hand with our heavenly Father in faith and obedience, we can trust God for protection from anything or anyone who would stand against us and threaten to cause us harm. God looks around us, places His hand against our chest and tells the world, "Don't you touch My son! Don't you threaten My daughter!" The safest place in the world is in the center of God's will.

Power—That mighty hand of God is a hand of power. Under that hand we have the power to overcome and defeat the circumstances and problems that come against us and place us in harm's way. Like a father who places his strong hand over the small, weak hand of his child to help him push an obstacle out of his way, God's powerful hand over ours assures us victory over the obstacles in our path.

You have heard the expression,
"Talk to the hand." Here's a new one:
"Get under the Hand!"

Purpose—God's hand points the way to His eternal purposes for our lives. When God stopped Saul of Tarsus and changed his destiny on the road to Damascus, He told Saul:

> Rise and stand on your feet; for I have appeared to you *for this purpose.*
>
> —ACTS 26:16, EMPHASIS ADDED

Wouldn't you love for God to arrest you on the path you have chosen for your life and change your destiny by saying, "I have appeared unto you for this purpose"? He will. And just as He told Paul what his new destiny was to be, God will reveal the purpose of your life to you.

Our fulfillment as Christians depends on fulfilling the purposes of God by the way we live our lives. By humbling ourselves under the mighty hand of God we can find those purposes. In 1 Peter we read:

> "God resists the proud, but gives grace to the humble." Therefore humble yourselves under the mighty hand of God, that He may exalt you in due time, casting all your care upon Him, for He cares for you.
>
> —1 Peter 5:5–7

One of the things that is clear from these verses is that *when you come under the mighty hand of God, the mighty hand of God comes under you.* The fulfilled and purpose-driven Christian life is one that is surrendered in humility to God. To walk this way as a disciple of Jesus Christ will cost you and I everything, but it also will provide everything that God has planned for your life and mine.

Living a Life That Works

Is your life working the way you think it should work? Are you satisfied with the results? The Christian life is supposed to work. I am not saying that it's supposed to be easy. I am not saying that it's without tribulation and hardship. But there are principles that God has clearly laid out in His Word that promise great blessing and great reward.

Let me say it again:
With God, life works!

When you look at your life, what do you see? Do you deal with the same issues over and over? Do you confront different people, different details, but arrive at the same unfulfilling results again and again? Have the plans you have created and followed for your life failed to bring you into the abundant life that Jesus talks about in John 10:10?

Let me say it again: With God, life works! God's mighty hand is reaching out to you. But you must look up to Him—not down at your circumstances. You must reach up—and loose your hold on the things of earth. You must grasp that mighty hand with all your might. Partner with God in a life so amazing you can't even imagine it, let alone ask for it.

God wants us to walk with Him because He loves us, He created us, He knows us and He wants us to know Him. He wants to use us, and He wants us to have lives filled with purpose and meaning. In Ephesians 1:15–21, the apostle Paul gives us a glimpse of what is in God's heart for us:

> I…do not cease…making mention of you in my prayers: that the God of our Lord Jesus Christ, the Father of glory, may give to you the spirit of wisdom and revelation in the knowledge of Him, the eyes of your understanding being enlightened; that you may know what is the hope of His calling, what are the riches of the glory of His inheritance in the saints, and what is the exceeding greatness of His power toward us who believe, according to the working of His mighty power which He worked in Christ when He raised Him from the dead and seated Him at His right hand in the heavenly places, far above all principality and power and might and dominion, and every name that is named, not only in this age but also in that which is to come.

When the apostle Paul prays in this chapter of Ephesians that you would "know" the hope of His calling, he uses the Greek word *ginosko*, which means "to know by experience." He is praying that you will experience what it means to have Jesus fulfill you in a way that surpasses anything you could ask or even imagine. Just think of that. Paul wants us to realize that God has plans for us, and they are always good, as Jeremiah 29:11 says:

> "For I know the plans I have for you," says the Lord, "plans for welfare and not for calamity to give you a future and a hope."
>
> —ASV

Are You Satisfied With the Results?

Do you wake up in the morning and think, *What is going to happen today?*—dreading the answer to that question? Do you reach the end of the day and think, *Oh, well, another day just like all the rest.* Do you long for significance, security and satisfaction? Those are the things that God longs to give to you. He wants you to spring to your feet each morning in anticipation of the blessing you will receive that day. He wants you to lay your head on your pillow at night fully satisfied with your day.

You may be lacking fulfillment and purpose in your life because you haven't properly submitted under the mighty hand of God. You might be saying, "It feels like there are a lot of things shifting and shaking around me, and I am uncomfortable." This may be your season for recognizing that God wants you to be under His mighty hand, to walk humbly with Him, to submit to both the process and the purposes He has for you.

Allowing God's hand to rest upon us may bring some discomfort. Have you ever watched a child squirming in his parent's hand? Staying under God's hand will require some change. As that mighty hand of God gently guides us in directions unfamiliar to us, we may feel like squirming out to return to more familiar times. But God wants to teach us how to remain in His zone of blessing. He wants to be our guide, our confidant, to walk with us every step of the way.

Do you long for significance, security and satisfaction? Those are the things that God longs to give to you.

God wants to deliver us from our attachment to the familiar. God desires to bring change into our lives. In fact, He wants to change us in such a deep and lasting way that we will be in power and ministry like the church He left here two thousand years ago.

To reach the destiny God has for you will require that you

learn to come under the mighty hand of God—not just once, but that you learn *to live* under the mighty hand of God. Submit to that hand when it gently restricts you from going where you think you want to go. Respond to that hand when it moves you in a new direction. Yield to that hand when it rests heavily upon you in correction. Obey that hand regardless of the way you feel.

Get fully under that mighty hand of God. You can't stay dry in a rainstorm by getting halfway under an umbrella. Being halfway under an umbrella is going to result in you being fully wet. Nor can you be halfway in the secret place of the Most High. God blesses complete submission.

The good news is, God is for you. He wants your Christian life to be one that works. And He knows it will, if you don't resist Him but submit yourself to His will and the good plan He has for you.

When You Feel Like Running, Run to God

Why would we not want to walk with our Creator in intimate fellowship, knowing that He wants to promote us, provide for us, protect us, empower us and give us purpose? Yet, not all of us want the kind of relationship with God that comes with radical submission to Him. We prefer a relationship that is based more on our terms than His.

Get fully under that mighty hand of God.

For some of us it is because our flesh and our will resist it, knowing that such a walk costs us. But we fail to think of how much more it costs us to live outside His will and purposes. Perhaps we are ignorant of His goodness and His promises. Others of us are inclined to trust in "things" or are inclined to trust in ourselves, or we are inclined to promote ourselves according to our own timetable, rather than letting God lift us up in His time, according to His will.

In 1 Peter we find that God wants us to walk humbly with Him as well as with one another. As Peter explains, walking with God means that He will exalt us to new things in His timing and that in the process we can believe—and this is the great news—that He cares for us and all that is connected to us:

> The elders who are among you I exhort, I who am a fellow elder and a witness of the sufferings of Christ, and also a partaker of the glory that will be revealed: Shepherd the flock of God which is among you, serving as overseers, not by compulsion but willingly, not for dishonest gain but eagerly; nor as being lords over those entrusted to you, but being examples to the flock; and when the Chief Shepherd appears, you will receive the crown of glory that does not fade away. Likewise you younger people, submit yourselves to your elders. Yes, all of you be submissive to one another, and be clothed with humility, for "God *resists* the *proud*, but gives *grace* to the *humble.*"
>
> Therefore humble yourselves under the mighty hand of God, that He may exalt you in due time, casting all your care upon Him, for He cares for you. Be sober, be vigilant; because your adversary the devil walks about like a roaring lion, seeking whom he may devour. Resist him, steadfast in the faith, knowing that the same sufferings are experienced by your brotherhood in the world.
>
> —1 PETER 5:1–9, EMPHASIS ADDED

The people to whom Peter wrote were going through tough, challenging times in their lives. Yet Peter encouraged them with the good news that God would exalt them in due time. "Cast your cares on Him," he urged them, "for He cares for your every need."

When we go through challenging times in our lives, one of the first things we're tempted to do is run and hide. We are tempted to withdraw from people, to get out from under biblical authority and maybe even to minimize the need for authority in our lives or to blame it for causing bad things to happen to us.

In effect, Peter was telling the people, "I am writing to tell you that these sufferings are being experienced by your brethren around the world. God is going to refine you and bring you forth from this like gold. Even in the midst of this, you can have joy—unspeakable joy—that is full of glory."

Peter told them what God expected of them, even in their difficulties:

> All of you be submissive to one another, and be clothed with humility for "God resists the proud, but gives grace to the humble." Therefore humble yourselves under the mighty hand of God, that He may exalt you in due time.
>
> —1 PETER 5:5–6

God was encouraging them to look ahead at His purpose—He wanted to lift them up at the right time to a place of wholeness, fruitfulness and greater influence.

HOW STRONG IS YOUR GOD?

King David had a radical devotion to God. On many occasions, he proved his commitment to God by placing it before the safety of his own life. One of those times occurred before he was king. He was just a young shepherd boy without military skills, yet David risked his life to fight Goliath, a champion warrior. This story reveals how the five life-giving attributes of God's mighty hand that we looked at earlier were at work in David's life. Because he had God's favor and approval, he experienced God's grace and blessing in each of these five areas:

Promotion—God promoted David by calling him out of the sheepfolds and anointing him at the hands of Samuel as the future king of Israel.

Provision—God provided David with every resource that he needed to defeat Goliath, which in this case happened to be a sling and a stone.

Protection—God protected David's life and spared him from Goliath's superior size and power.

Power—God gave David supernatural power to prevail over Goliath.

Purpose—God's hand of purpose pointed the way for David's encounter with Goliath and from that point forward—ultimately leading to David's fulfilling his God-given destiny as the king of Israel.

Even though God is not calling most of us (if any of us!) literally to fight the kind of battle that David had to fight that day, He does want us to understand that His mighty hand—with the same five attributes that delivered David—is extended toward us today. God wants to be just as strong on your behalf and my behalf as He was on David's behalf.

God is extending an invitation for us to live a radically committed life for Him. The choice is ours.

According to His Word, His will for any of us who want to walk with Him is to humble ourselves under His mighty hand and wait for Him to exalt us, to appoint us to new things according to His purposes. I believe this is His will for all Christians.

How strong is your God? Is He as strong in your life as He was in David's? If He isn't, He wants you to submit yourself under His hand, where He can strengthen you, fill you with purpose and lift you up at the right time. That's the kind of Christian life He wants you to have.

Come Fully Under the Mighty Hand of God

The term *submit* means to willingly come under authority—both God's authority and man's. Ultimately, the authority we must live under is God's authority because that's the way Jesus lived. Jesus said He only did what He saw the Father doing and only said what He heard the Father saying (John 5:19). And in His actions He was 100 percent accurate, 100 percent of the time.

You and I will never hit it 100 percent of the time the way Jesus did, because we know and see only in part. But our goal should be to please God in everything. I want to please God 100 percent of the time. And even though I have never had a week, or even a day, that I could say was "perfect," that is my goal, and for all of us that should be our pursuit.

Humbling ourselves under the mighty hand of God is a choice we have to make. We have to choose to come under God's hand and under the hand of those in spiritual authority who are, in fact, God's hands extended to us.

We submit to one another in many different ways. But if we resist God's authority in our lives, God will ultimately resist us.

You will discover that the reason you have not been fully released in your Christian life is because you have harbored a seed of rebellion against God's authority in your life. You do not really trust that God truly has your best interest at heart, so you try to take matters into your own hands.

God is extending an invitation for us to live a radically committed life for Him. The choice is ours.

This is pride. And the problem with pride is that it lifts us up and brings God down—which ultimately then makes us God in our own lives. If we are in charge, then we become our own gods. If we are the ones who are saying, "I'm going to do whatever I want, and this and that is going to happen," then we have lifted ourselves to the level of God.

Either we are going to let God be God, or we are going to be God. And if you or I want to be God, then it won't go well for us—God is not willing to share His glory with anyone. But each of us has to make that decision. To submit to God means to come under His authority—in everything. God resists the proud, but He gives favor and blessing to the humble.

The fact that men and women—imperfect people of flesh and blood who are flawed like you and me—occupy positions of spiritual authority means that sometimes people get hurt. That is an unfortunate reality.

Are You Practicing "Selective Submission"?

It oftentimes is in this "flesh and blood" arena of relationships where submission seems for some of us to be the hardest test we face. Have you ever heard someone say—or maybe you've said it yourself: "I'm not putting up with this anymore. I've had it. I'm gone. I'm outta here."

I think Christians who say that are underestimating the fact that God takes our walk with Him more seriously than we do.

We overlook a fact of the Christian life, which is this: When we have enough junk in our lives, God may choose to let things go wrong in order to work into our lives some things that are right.

But we who are new creations in Christ should *want* to get this thing right. We should want to honor God. We should want to do what the Lord wants us to do. We should say about whatever He chooses to have us go through, "Lord, bring it on—because I know that Your plans for me are good."

Nothing is more essential to the success of our Christian lives than our being fully submitted to the will and the ways of God. Yet we often find ourselves practicing what I would call *selective submission.* We love God, we want to follow Him, we want to fellowship with Him and we call him Lord, but do we walk with Him humbly, as our Lord and our God?

In our family, we have a little dog, Christie, who practices *serious* selective submission.

She's a purebred French Bichon Frise with a real attitude. In trying to teach this dog to obey, I would become increasingly frustrated. In her own way, she was independent, stubborn and rebellious. I would tell her, "No, Christie!" and she would gaze up at me with what looked like trusting, understanding eyes—and then go right back to disobeying me. I would win the battle for obedience in one area of behavior only to lose it in another area.

One day as I tried to get her to obey what I was telling her, the Lord used her as a very vivid picture of how I oftentimes relate to Him.

That little dog in her selective submission was a picture of how I can walk in selective submission. The same dog that often rebels against me wants to lick my hand and come up in the chair and sit next to me and show me her love. Yet there is still a streak of rebellion in her, and she wants to have her own way. How often that has been true in my own life, and perhaps yours. On one hand we love Jesus and want to be next to Him. Yet on the other hand, we do not obey Him in each and every circumstance.

But she is an animal, and we are new creations in Christ. And so we have the capacity to learn more and more of what it means to bring our lives under the lordship of Christ.

I think this an important word for the Lord's church to grasp. As an American I can say that in my country, dubbed as "The Land of the Free" and "The Home of the Brave," we really struggle with this concept because we are fed so much a belief system that says we are free to do whatever we want, whenever we want, as long as we don't break the laws of the land. But I have discovered that whoever we are and wherever we live, as people we tend to think that we can do whatever we want.

Unbelievers can do whatever they want, but the people of God are to do whatever *He* wants. We see people living the life that we want to live, and we think, *That it is the life that I am supposed to have*, only to find out after we have pursued it that it isn't really what we wanted or what we needed. But the truth is, every one of us who is a Christian is called to be a full-time disciple, fully submitted to God's will and purposes. There is an eternal destiny for every one of our lives; there is a God-ordained plan, there is a God-designed process, there is a God-supplied product that He wants to bring us into and accomplish in each of us.

Receiving that reality depends on humbling ourselves under the mighty hand of God. When we go our own way, we find out that—as far as God's path is concerned—our way is the wrong way.

God knows what His highest and best is for each of us, and whether we selectively obey Him or assume that we know what is best for us, we will miss abiding under the mighty hand of God and finding His will for our lives

Great News: The Longing for Success and Significance Is a Godly Desire

If we are serious about being submitted under God's hand, we should remember that it isn't wrong for us to assume that because God made us in His own image we are pretty important to Him. The fact that He did not spare His own Son shows us just how high a price He was willing to pay to bring us back into relationship with Him.

I have great news for you: That longing you have to feel significant, to experience success in your Christian life and to feel that you serve an important role in God's plan is a godly desire.

Years after Adam and Eve first walked with God in the Garden of Eden, God called Abraham His "friend" because Abraham believed God and obeyed Him. When Abraham obeyed God and offered his son Isaac on the altar of sacrifice—before God stopped him and provided a ram in place of Isaac—God affirmed Abraham as a righteous man. (See James 2:21–23.) As a result, God blessed Abraham with significance and purpose and told him he would be "the father of many nations."

God took a disenfranchised and seemingly insignificant Moabite woman named Ruth and joined her in marriage to Boaz, a leader in Israel. Their marriage furthered the lineage of King David, which led to the birth of Jesus, the promised Messiah.

God's purpose for Ruth wasn't just for her to marry a bigwig in Israel. His purpose also was for her to have a significant part in the fulfillment of His plan to provide the Messiah. Even though Ruth wasn't a Jew, God provided her with a place of significance by choosing her and showing that He had preordained for Jesus to be the Savior of the Gentiles as well as the Jews.

The Feeble Hand of Man vs. The Mighty Hand of God

Many Christians seem forever to be talking about what we will or won't do. We call ourselves followers of Christ, yet we talk about His will for us as if it's optional—as if it really is something we can take or leave.

The fact of the matter is, not only is God's will not optional, but it also lifts us up to the highest possible place of fruitful ministry in any given season in our lives—if we will allow God to place us there by His hand.

Now, that's a relative concept because some people have a larger place of ministry and influence than other people. We don't need to envy people who have a larger ministry, and we don't need to feel insignificant if ours is smaller.

The principle then is clear.
When you come under the mighty hand of God,
the mighty hand of God comes under you.

What we need to do as we come under God's mighty hand is to trust that He lifts us up to the right place at the right time to do the right things with the right people. Whatever God lifts you up to—at whatever point He lifts you up—will be a privilege because it is God who put you there.

The mighty hand of God never fails. It has power for this life and for the life to come.

If man lifts you up, man will eventually let you down. But if God lifts you up, He is able to keep you up. He might reassign you or put you in another place, but He will keep you up. When God puts you in a place of His choosing, only He can take you out of that place. Man cannot.

The principle then is clear. When you come under the

mighty hand of God, the mighty hand of God comes under you. The feeble hand of man will lift you up as far as it can, but it will fail you. People around you who are supposedly "making" you will fail you. That boss in whom you are putting so much confidence because he has made you promises will, at some point, fail you.

The hand of man makes promises, but they are promises that can't always be kept. When God makes a promise, He is able to deliver on it. So do not submit yourself under the feeble hand of man. Submit yourself under the mighty hand of God.

That hand will never allow a promise He has made to you to be broken. As you learn to trust that hand, your spirit will soar to new heights of confidence and security. You will experience the life you have always longed to live. The dreams and visions you have had of a destiny you had never before realized will begin to take place in your life under that hand. Living under the mighty hand of God is your destiny—it's your birthright.

As we will see in the chapters to come, God's hand is a hand of promotion, provision, protection, power and purpose. When you submit yourself to God you get all this and more.

We Look to You, Jesus

We look to You, Jesus.
Revive us, our King.
Come show us Your glory;
Come do a new thing.

We look to You, Jesus.
Your will, our desire.
Lord, send forth Your power
And fill us with Your fire.

—Lyrics by Dale Evrist and Gary Sadler

Chapter 2

Living by Prophetic Assignment

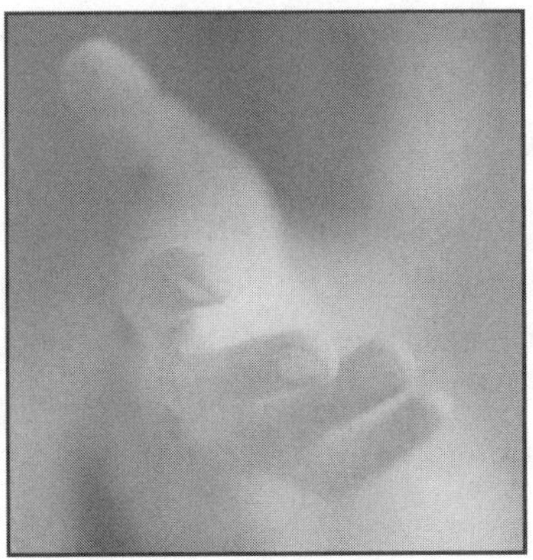

"Why do I keep coming around to the same mountain time and time again?" "Why do I continue to bump up against the same obstacles over and over again?" "Why do I have the sense in my heart that there is a plan and purpose for my life that never seems to be realized?" Have you ever asked these questions?

Sometimes we find ourselves frustrated and unhappy because we are in the wrong place—we are not where God has placed us. Instead, we are where we have placed ourselves. But God has a specific place for you—and it's a good place. You do not have to bump from place to place…job to job…relationship to relationship. The Father longs to guide you, to steer you into just the right place. He has a *prophetic assignment* just for you.

The Father longs to be in dialogue with you to such an extent that if you veer to the right or to the left of His chosen place for you, you will hear His voice gently but firmly saying, "This is the way; walk in it." He wants you to be able to feel the subtle pressure of His mighty hand changing your course at the slightest step off His path.

But this kind of radical relationship with God does not come automatically. We must be willing to adjust our steps...heed His warning...and crucify thinking patterns that were formed when we were walking in the paths of our own choices. If we fail to do these things, we will stumble out of the place God has for us and back into the paths of our own sinful choices.

> My people...have stumbled off the ancient highways of good, and they walk the muddy paths of sin. Therefore, their land will become desolate, a monument to their stupidity. All who pass by will be astonished and shake their heads in amazement at its utter desolation.
>
> —Jeremiah 18:15–16, nlt

God's Will: Hearing and Doing

Have you ever asked a child, "Honey, what do you want to be when you grow up?" While that might seem like a perfectly normal question to ask a child, do you know that's really the wrong question to ask if you are a disciple of Jesus Christ and seeking to raise up disciples of Jesus Christ? A better question would be, "Son, are you getting any sense of what God may be calling you to when you get older?" Or, "Honey, I'm praying for you. I know that you are just a little girl right now, but I'm praying that God will help you fulfill His dream for your life."

God has a specific place for you—
and it's a good place.

God's purpose for us—not our own wants—should determine our destiny. I know...I know...you'll say, "But the Bible says that God wants to give me the desires of my heart." But if you really look closely at the passages that teach that, you will find out that God gives us the desires of our heart when we allow our heart to be aligned with His heart and when His desires become our desires. When we say to our kids, "What do you want to be when you grow up?", we are taking their focus off what God might want to do with their lives.

When asked that question, a boy may respond, "Well, I want to be a fireman."

"I want to be a ballerina," a girl might say.

When we ask our children what they want to do with their lives, at a very early age we create in them the thinking that whatever they want to do is OK—it's their choice!

But that is not discipleship—it's putting man's will at the center of the universe. That's the root of humanism. God's will should be at the center of our lives.

Prophetic assignment is living our lives by the assignment God gives us. "Where, Lord? Where would You have me go? How would You have me live?" are the questions we ask if we are truly living by prophetic assignment. Again, what we are saying, and what is the essence of living by prophetic assignment, is that we are at the right place, at the right time, with the right people, doing the right things.

Don't let the word *prophetic* scare you off—it just means that God has spoken to you and shown you in some way what He is calling or has called you to do in your life.

Living by prophetic assignment is contrary to living by self-motivated direction. It ultimately is the difference between *discipleship* and *lordship*. Prophetic assignment means that at all times our direction in life is surrendered to God: "Whatever You say, Lord, that's what I say. Whatever You want me to do, Lord, that's what I will do."

Living by prophetic assignment means that we ask those kind of questions of God and then live by obeying what He says.

God's Call: Doing What He Is Blessing

Many Christians have failed to live by prophetic assignment. Many live their lives according to a skewed gospel that says, "Whatever man wants to do for God he can, and God is bound to bless what he does."

How about you? Have you been snared by such skewed thinking? Let's see how this might happen. We have something we want to do. It sounds good to us—it's not illegal, immoral or fattening (or at least two of the three mentioned!). So we just do it. We don't ask God. We don't seek God. We don't wait for God—*we just do it!*

Then when it doesn't work, we start to pray, "O God, bless this." "O God, *please* bless this." Soon we are praying, "O God, please, please, please bless this! If You don't, I'm in a lot of trouble!"

Too late. God is not bound to bless what we are doing—we are bound to do what He is blessing. Just making this single thought shift can make all the difference in your life.

The Bible says that Jesus did whatever He saw His Father doing:

> I say to you, the Son can do nothing of Himself, but what He sees the Father do; for whatever He does, the Son also does in like manner.
>
> —John 5:19

Jesus said *and did* what He saw the Father saying and doing. That's the way you and I need to live our lives. Whatever we see God doing, that's what we do. Whatever we hear God saying, that's what we say.

Practicing Righteousness

My wife, Joan, and I have lived that way for years—not perfectly, of course—because we're still in the process of growing. I am still prone to do foolish things—but my commitment is not to do foolish things. "To do as many foolish things as I can in a lifetime" is not part of my personal mission statement. I am really trying not to practice my mistakes.

It's like when you are learning how to play a guitar; you practice by following your instructor's method and trying to do it right. You will make mistakes, but you are not practicing your mistakes. You are learning from your mistakes—not doing the same foolish thing over and over again. You are practicing how to do it right.

In our lives, Joan and I are practicing righteousness. That is what we are after—God's righteousness. The very reason our church, New Song Christian Fellowship, exists is because Joan and I believe in living by prophetic assignment. That's why we are pastoring in Nashville instead of entering into what would be our seventeenth year of ministry at our former church in Southern California.

"To do as many foolish things as I can in a lifetime" is not part of my mission statement.

We are in our eighth year of ministry here at New Song because we got under the mighty hand of God and said, "Wherever You tell us to go, that's where we'll go, Lord. Whatever You tell us to do, that's what we'll do." And as a result, God brought us to Nashville.

A question for you might be, "Where is God calling you?"

Do Not Confuse Talent and Calling

When I lived in Southern California I knew a man who had a powerful gift of evangelism. If you heard him speak and saw him minister, you would assume that God would have given him a large platform from which to use his powerful evangelistic gifts. What was interesting about him is that what he did day by day is deliver the mail. He was a mailman. When he would ask God how to make sense of this incredible passion he had to win the lost, with his day-to-day job of being a mailman, God assured him that he was at the right place, at the right time, with the right people, doing the right thing.

Over the years countless scores of men and women came to Christ as this man who had dedicated his life to the Lord delivered the mail. But more than that, he delivered the good news of the saving power of Jesus Christ.

You can never go wrong in answering God's call—even if it seems that what you are doing is simply delivering the mail.

The point is that some of us look at our lives in Christ as if the better money or better opportunity determines God's will for us. Somebody shows you the money, and you bolt for the door.

Do not confuse talent or opportunity with calling.

That's confusing your *talents* (and what they can do for you) with your *calling* (what God has planned for you). It is confusing an *opportunity* with a *calling*. That is not living by prophetic assignment. That is you assuming, "Well, this is all about better opportunities for me. People can see I'm talented, gifted in this or that, and they're offering me the kind of opportunity I probably deserve."

However, if you live by your talents alone, be aware that the nature of men will be to push and push, rush and rush if they find a talent in you they can use to their advantage. Often, men will want to put you right in the middle of something that your character may not be able to handle and that may not be consistent with your calling. Then, in many cases, they will watch you spiral down in flames.

They will talk about you and say, "Wasn't that a shame? What happened?"

For your sake, you had better be sure God is the one who is releasing you into anything that you do or claim to be doing for Him. Just because a person is talented or well-known at being gifted at something does not mean he or she should be doing it.

Do not confuse talent or opportunity with calling. Just

because you can does not mean you should.

I have known people who had the talent to become huge at what they did, and yet God gave them a small sphere in which to function. They said, "Yes, God," to what He wanted for them at the expense of doing with their lives what they probably knew they had the talent to do. I have known gifted people in my life who, if you could have seen them doing what they were talented at, you would have wondered why you had never heard of them.

There is a man in our church who is an incredibly gifted singer and songwriter. Everyone, from the time he began, told him that he was destined for a national platform. As the years went on, he enjoyed some success, but it seemed that God continued to call him to a smaller sphere and platform. This was confusing, both to him and to those around him.

One day in my office we talked about this. I asked him the question, "Would it be all right for God to take someone of your talent and ability and give you away to a smaller group of people just because He loved those people that much?"

This man responded, "Absolutely, that would be fine with me."

It is amazing to see how this man now goes into small venues and blesses handfuls of people who, with tears of gratitude, come up at the end of the evening and say, "I can't believe that you came, but I'm so glad you did." That is going by calling rather than talent and opportunity.

So when you ask the questions, "Why weren't they better known?" "Why didn't they have a larger platform?", often the answer is because they did not confuse talent with calling. God gave them as a gift to a certain community of people who were within their sphere of influence, and they accepted that as the limit of God's calling for them, willing to stay put unless God gave them more. Let me ask you a question: "Would it be OK with you if God took you—with your considerable talents—and chose to give you away to a group of people who were smaller, but every bit as important, to Him?" You are part of that Abrahamic covenant. That means that you have access to the blessings God promised to Abraham.

> I will establish My covenant between Me and you and your descendants after you in their generations, for an everlasting covenant, to be God to you and your descendants after you. Also I give to you and your descendants after you the land in which you are a stranger, all the land of Canaan, as an everlasting possession; and I will be their God.
>
> —GENESIS 17:7–8

Have you possessed your Canaan? God wants to bless you to make you a blessing, and He wants to make your name "great"—whether your greatness is known to the multitudes or to God alone—but there are varying degrees to that. And if we confuse talent with calling, then we will fail to realize that real promotion in God comes from living by prophetic assignment.

There have been a lot of books written about church growth. Most of them have to do with how to get your church to grow rapidly. There is a well-respected pastor in our city who has been pastoring in the same church for fifty years. For years and years, while being a very fruitful ministry in our community, the church he pastors was certainly not one of the largest churches. He was happy and content to pastor whatever people God gave him.

There came a point in his ministry where God chose to take that church from a medium-sized ministry that was very fruitful to a huge ministry that had a national platform. It has been remarkable to see this very humble and godly man go from a place of being willing to pastor dozens, then hundreds, on to pastoring thousands and then to become a pastor to pastors. It is a great illustration of how, if we will humble ourselves under the mighty hand of God, we just can never tell what God might do.

Some of us seem to think that there are saints like Mother Teresa who had to live according to a calling, and then there are people like us who live according to our preferences. But that is not true.

It is all about calling. It is all about assignment. It is all about discerning and doing what God has given you to do.

Decisions vs. Determinations

We often hear believers say, "I have so many big decisions to make." From what I have read in Scripture, that is really not the case. We have one big decision to make—that we are going to do whatever God tells us to do. We say, "Whatever You want, Lord. That is what I want."

That is the decision Jesus Christ made. Jesus came to earth by the authority and the will of the Father—not by His own authority. It was His Father, Almighty God, who determined the three-and-a-half-year time frame when He would minister on earth and then suffer an agonizing death to atone for the sins of the world.

In the Garden of Gethsemane we see Jesus' agony as He prays. It is clear from His words that He has already decided that He would do whatever His Father said. Three times He prayed, "O My Father, if it is possible, let this cup pass from Me; nevertheless, not as I will, but as You will" (Matt. 26:39). That's *determination language*—it is not *decision language!*

I remember one of my Bible college professors saying that in that moment, Jesus was saying, "If someone can believe in Buddha and be saved, I'm not going to the cross. If someone can believe in Krishna and be saved, I'm not going to the cross. If fighting in a world war, paying taxes and obeying the government earns a person enough points to be saved, then I'm not going to the cross. But if there is no other way—if this really is Your will, Father—then I will do whatever it is You have determined for Me to do!"

That's the difference between a decision and a determination. The *decision* we make is to say, "I'm going to obey God." Period! The *determinations* we make happen as we consider the right place to be, the right time to be there, the right people to be with and the right things to do.

Living by determination is liberating. It removes the cumbersome weight of feeling, "Oh my gosh, I have so many decisions to make in my life." We do not have many decisions to make—all we need is to make the Lord decision maker of our lives. Then we can say, "I've already decided to follow God. Now I'm determining to get before God, read His Word and listen to His voice. Then I will know His will for my life."

Living As a Disciple Instead of Living As a Lord

In order for our lives to find true fulfillment in God, we need to live by prophetic assignment. It is the key to God's power operating in our lives because it will help us avoid the errors that come from living by our own whims. And it will help us secure our God-given destiny.

For example, if we believe God is God and Jesus is Lord, then we won't run around saying, "I have two years left before I retire, and when I do, I've always had a dream of going and doing such and such a thing. And I tell you what, when I work that last week, and I go to that retirement dinner and am really retired, we're selling the house and packing up and heading off to..."—you name the place.

I am sorry, but that is not what disciples do.

"You mean to tell me," you ask, "that after working my whole life I cannot retire wherever I want to? I can't just say I want to be close to my grandkids, so I'm going to move there?"

Sure, you can do that. But it does not necessarily mean that if you do, you are going to be in God's will. But you can do whatever you want.

"I can do whatever I want. Will God still love me?"

Of course.

"Will I still be saved?"

Absolutely. But you may be missing something incredibly

wonderful that God has for you. You may not realize it, and you may not find out about it until you stand at the judgment seat of Christ—but you will miss it because you took matters into your own hands and led with your heart rather than with your spirit.

"Well, I just missed my grandkids, and I wanted to be closer to them."

That's legitimate. But the question is not whether you want to live closer to your grandkids. The question is what Jesus wants to do in your life. What does Jesus want to do with you now that you are no longer working every day?

My mom and dad don't live close to their grandchildren—my kids. My mom and dad live twenty-three hundred miles away from Nashville because that is God's will for them. And I took their grandkids twenty-three hundred miles away because that was God's will for my family.

Joan and I aren't raising our children to stay close by us. If each of us were asked, we might say, "Yes, that's what I would hope for." But more than anything, we are raising our children to be disciplined, devoted followers of the Lord Jesus Christ. Family matters can ruin the will of God quicker than just about anything, if you let them.

You will start saying, "Oh, I feel the tug of the Lord to go here, but I can't leave my mom and dad. I can't leave my brothers and sisters. I can't leave my nieces and nephews," and before you know it, God's will is far less important to you than your family.

To follow in the path of God's prophetic assignment for our lives, we must learn to trust God with our families. I know of one lady who was contemplating if a move with her family of more than fifteen hundred miles away from her terminally ill parents could possibly be God's prophetic assignment for her. She traveled with her husband to interview for the new position—even though at the very time she was there her father was in the hospital recovering from a heart attack brought on by his disease of congestive heart failure. Her mother had already been diagnosed with terminal cancer. As she agonized alone in prayer in a motel room one morning, she asked God, "How can You ask me to do this? How can I leave my parents and move fifteen hundred miles away from them?" Immediately she felt arms—an actual sense of the physical touch of arms—placed around her. Believing her husband had entered the room and was comforting her, she looked up to thank him. But no one was there. Then, in her spirit, she heard God's voice comforting her with these words: "I'll take care of you—and your parents. Trust Me and follow My path for your lives."

Real faith ultimately flows out of submission to the living God and whatever plans He has for our lives.

That's how prophetic assignment works. God works out every detail in response to your willingness to completely submit to His plan for your life.

Jesus was willing to trust His Father with His earthly family. Jesus had to leave Nazareth so that He could fulfill His mission to be the Savior of the world. And He left willingly. There was nothing in biblical prophecy that showed the Messiah conducting His ministry in Nazareth or laying down His life in His hometown. Nazareth was not meant to be the centerpiece of God's redemptive purposes in Jesus. Even as Jesus was a devoted follower of the will and ways of God the Father, so we are to be, and to raise our children to be, devoted followers of the will and ways of God the Father and our Lord Jesus Christ.

ORDERING OUR STEPS

Joan and I know that God is a provider, and He is not going to lead us somewhere and then abandon us there. When it comes to our children, we are not raising them with the idea that, "When you grow up and get married, you're not going anywhere because we want to have you around."

I know of a pastor (who will remain nameless) who, when his daughters were wanting to get married, would bring prospective suitors in and give them a talk. Now, this is a man who preaches faith—as much as any person I know.

He would bring young men in and say, "I would be willing to consider you as a possible husband for my daughter with this understanding: You do not leave this church, you do not leave this community, you do not take my daughter away and you do not take away my grandchildren that will come.

"If you're going to be my son-in-law, you're going to stay here in this church, because I'm going to have my family around me. Now if you can marry with that understanding, I would be open to having you in the family."

Can you imagine that? You see, it doesn't matter how big your name is, how big your church is, whether you've written books, whether you appear on television, whether you preach faith above anything else. None of those things matter because real faith ultimately flows out of submission to the living God and whatever plans He has for our lives and in finding that we must order our steps according to what He says, not what men say.

Learning to order our steps according to God's plans for our lives—not our own—demonstrates real faith.

> But the path of the just is like the shining sun, that shines ever brighter unto the perfect day. The way of the wicked is like darkness: they do not know what makes them stumble.
>
> —Proverbs 4:18–19

Disciplined to Devotion

If we violate the principle of prophetic assignment, then to one degree or another we will miss our destiny. We will simply miss it.

Most believers, unfortunately, never fully realize their destiny. I do not mean they are not saved, and I don't mean they do not realize their ultimate destiny of being with God forever.

But they do not attain their purpose in God simply because they do not come under the mighty hand of God. They often live under the feeble hand of man. They are the captain of their own destiny.

They say, "I'm going to do this; I'm going to do that. We're going to move here; we're going to go there. I'm going to work here; I'm going to work there. I'm going to go to school here. After I get out of school, we're going to do this and that and the other thing."

And they think that God is honor-bound to bless what they are doing. But He isn't.

As a pastor, I do not want to see anyone miss his or her destiny in God. I want to hear it said of you when you stand before the Lord, "Well done, good and faithful servant… Enter into the joy of your Lord" (Matt. 25:21). (Notice He didn't say "good and faithful *master* or *lord*"!)

Enter into the joy of "your Lord."

You know, the people to whom God is going to say, "Well done," are the people who lived under Him as their Lord, who came under the mighty hand of God, who let God determine His purpose for them, who let God place them with people who could speak His will into their lives. They live by prophetic assignment.

Come under the mighty hand of God, and the mighty hand of God will come under you. What better place could there be for you than the place God chooses for you? Even if it's a hard place, as long as He is there, it's right. Even if it's a tough season, even if it's a trial, if you know the mighty hand of God is there, then you know the hand that put you there will keep you while you are there, show you your reason for being there and provide you with everything you need.

William Carey is often called the Father of Modern Missions. Shortly after the Baptist Missionary Society was formed in 1792, Carey volunteered to travel to India to serve the people there. With his wife and three small children he settled in a malaria-infested marsh outside Calcutta. Housing, food supplies and health care were utterly inadequate. Only the overpowering sense that he was accomplishing the will of God provided the staying power for Carey during his early years in India. After seven years of struggling to establish a ministry—which included language study, itinerant preaching and secular employment at an indigo factory—Carey was unable to claim even one Indian convert. But he knew that the hand that put him there was keeping him there. "I can plod, I can persevere in any definite pursuit," he wrote in his journal. And because he did, he eventually made a monumental contribution to missions by turning the tide of Protestant thought in favor of foreign missions. During his four decades of ministry in India, many new mission boards were organized and great missionary pioneers were penetrating the barriers of civilizations that were virtually unknown to the West. William Carey came under the mighty hand of God, and as a result, he experienced the awesome power of that mighty hand of God as it came under him.[1]

Promotion, provision, protection, power and purpose—all are there when we come under and submit ourselves to the mighty hand of God. They are all waiting for us at our assignment. And prophetic assignment is one of the keys to bringing ourselves under the mighty hand of God. The other, as we will see in the next chapter, is living in proper alignment.

---

1. John D. Woodbridge, ed., *Great Leaders of the Christian Church* (Chicago, IL: The Moody Bible Institute of Chicago, 1988), s.v. William Carey.

Run With the Righteous

Run with the righteous,
Run for the Call.
Running together,
Forsaking all.

No stopping, no stumbling,
No straying in sin.
Run with the righteous,
Run 'til you win.

—Lyrics by Dale Evrist

Chapter 3

Living in Proper Alignment

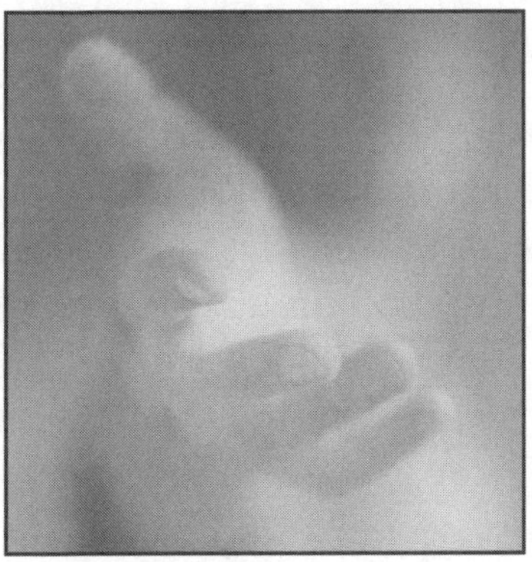

The second key for bringing our lives under the mighty hand of God is to live in *proper alignment.* Proper alignment means to come under God's authority in all of its expressions. Your purpose ultimately flows out of your submission to the living God and whatever He has for your life, whatever He wants to do with your life, whatever calling He places on your life.

Alignment: God's Call on Us All

Proper alignment also means that we must become properly aligned under spiritual authority, since God works through delegated authority. God wants us to align ourselves in relationships with people who can be part of God's voice as He speaks into our lives. This means that we are living in a correct relationship with God and with those who are in spiritual authority over us, those who are our spiritual peers and those who spiritually are under us.

We are always to ask the questions: "Who is over us?" "Who is next to us?" "Who is under us?"

If you are a person in authority, you must also be submissive to authority.

For many of us this is easier said than done. Perhaps you have been abused by authority. I do not mean to trivialize your experience or your pain, but each of us faces this as part of the human race and life as we know it! Each and every one of us has known, in one way or another, what it means to experience the abuse of authority. It varies in its painfulness, but inevitably it always hurts. But we need to understand that there is no Plan B.

However, being submitted to authority does not mean you are submitted to everyone—or to just anyone. It means being submitted to those leaders whom God has put over you, knowing that they will make mistakes and, most assuredly, will even disappoint you. But the mighty hand of God will protect, promote, prosper, empower and position you as you submit—even through the mistakes of those in authority over you.

Proper alignment is important because it flows down from the head of the church—Jesus Christ—to leaders He has placed within the body of Christ to help you. If you are a person in authority, you must also be submissive to authority. Leaders are not lords. Our Lord is Jesus. Leaders represent the Lord and, therefore, should be humble under the mighty hand of God.

Submitted to One Another

We submit to one another in many different ways. But if we resist God's authority in our lives, God will ultimately resist us. Humbling ourselves under the mighty hand of God is a choice we have to make. We must choose to come under God's hand

and under the hand of those in spiritual authority who are, in fact, God's hands extended to us.

There is no greater example of someone submitting under the mighty hand of God than Jesus Himself. He was totally submissive to God the Father, knowing that His Father would perfect His will in Him and raise Him up accordingly. The attitude of Jesus' heart, as seen in Philippians 2, is an example for us of the attitude we must develop in our own hearts.

> Let this mind be in you which was also in Christ Jesus, who, being in the form of God, did not consider it robbery to be equal with God, but made Himself of no reputation, taking the form of a bondservant, and coming in the likeness of men. And being found in appearance as a man, He humbled Himself and became obedient to the point of death, even the death of the cross. Therefore God also has highly exalted Him and given Him the name which is above every name, that at the name of Jesus every knee should bow, of those in heaven, and of those on earth, and of those under the earth, and that every tongue should confess that Jesus Christ is Lord, to the glory of God the Father.
>
> —Philippians 2:5–11

Profound Humility

We live in a profoundly proud generation. There is little true humility to be found anywhere. It is not profound pride that is required to please God—it is profound humility. All of us are going to have to make a decision as to whether or not we will get low before God and come under His mighty hand, exercising the kind of profound humility that enables God to be able to use us in an unlimited fashion.

One of the great signs of someone walking in humility is a person who can "own" his or her mistakes and sins. A truly humble man or woman willingly searches his or her heart and, by the grace of God, says the words that need to be said—"I'm sorry," "I was wrong" and "Please forgive me." God helps us when we humble ourselves before Him. Repentance is much easier than you think because the hand of God lifts you up and helps you when you humble yourself.

It is not profound pride that is required to please God—it is profound humility.

The call to "be clothed with humility" is for all, young and old, male and female. As we pray and ask the Lord to show us the places in our lives where we need to humble ourselves, He will teach us to wear the garments of humility.

The humble will submit to God and exalt God's abilities infinitely above their own, being completely dependent on the Lord. "It's all about You, Lord," they say. In contrast, the proud are presumptuous, boastful and self-reliant.

God Resists the Proud

As the people of God, at the very core of the things that we value should be the belief that God stands against the proud; He resists, frustrates and opposes the proud. If we are proud, God in His mercy may give us a period of time in which He deals with us. But ultimately that time will end, and God will begin to oppose us if we remain proud. There are many believers who find themselves rebuking the demonic when they need to be repenting of the pride in their own hearts. When God resists us, if we are not careful we will attribute the divine hand of God to the demonic hand of the enemy. We need to understand that the divine hand of God is resisting us unto repentance. When the demonic hand is attacking us, it is unto rebuking. If God resists us, He will win.

This principle can be clearly seen in God's dealings with King Saul. Saul had been handpicked by God to reign as the first king over Israel. Yet Saul was a proud man—too proud to humble himself under God and be obedient in all things.

At one point, God instructs Saul to attack Amalek and his

people and to "utterly destroy all that they have...kill both man and woman, infant and nursing child, ox and sheep, camel and donkey" (1 Sam. 15:3). But Saul resisted God's instructions to him. Although he attacked the Amalekites, he saw an opportunity to gather their wealth and possessions for himself, so he spared their livestock and took their king hostage.

God was so angered with Saul's disobedience that He told Samuel, "I greatly regret that I have set up Saul as king, for he has turned back from following Me, and has not performed My commandments" (v. 11). He instructed Samuel to go to Saul and confront him with his disobedience.

If God resists us, He will win.

Yet even when confronted by Samuel, Saul refused to acknowledge his pride. So God had no other choice but to oppose Saul because of his pride. Samuel delivered God's judgment upon Saul:

> Has the Lord as great delight in burnt offerings and sacrifices, as in obeying the voice of the LORD?...Because you have rejected the word of the LORD, He also has rejected you from being king.
>
> —1 SAMUEL 15:22–23

Saul lost his kingdom because of his pride and disobedience. Pride can infect any of us. It was pride that caused Satan to fall from his exalted position in heaven.

God resists the proud, but He gives grace to the humble. The word *resist* means "to oppose, to stand against, to frustrate." God is against the proud—those who are saying to Him, "I will do whatever I want to do."

So how can we avoid the temptation to become proud? We can accept the fact that we are never going to fully avoid pride. But each time we repent of pride and get our hearts right before God, we become better and better at avoiding pride. God's Word gives us the solution to our struggles with pride.

In 1 Peter 5:6 we are instructed to "humble yourselves under the mighty hand of God, that He may exalt you in due time." The wonderful news is that God gives grace when we choose to humble ourselves under His authority.

The People Over, Next to and Under You

As we live our lives in proper alignment, God uses the people He has placed in our lives as conduits for revealing His prophetic assignment to us.

> The elders who are among you I exhort, I who am a fellow elder and a witness of the sufferings of Christ, and also a partaker of the glory that will be revealed: Shepherd the flock of God which is among you, serving as overseers, not by compulsion but willingly, not for dishonest gain but eagerly; nor as being lords over those entrusted to you, but being examples to the flock; and when the Chief Shepherd appears, you will receive the crown of glory that does not fade away. Likewise you younger people, submit yourselves to your elders. Yes, all of you be submissive to one another, and be clothed with humility, for "God resists the proud, but gives grace to the humble." Therefore humble yourselves under the mighty hand of God, that He may exalt you in due time, casting all your care upon Him, for He cares for you.
>
> —1 Peter 5:1–7

God is perfect, and His perfect will can be done in your life and mine if we honor the structures of delegated authority that He has designed and put in place. The simplest way for us to do that is by surrendering our lives entirely to God.

As we learn to live in complete surrender to the will and ways of God, He will begin to teach us to live in proper alignment with the people around us. There are three ways we relate to people.

- An upward way of relating—the way we relate to the people who are over us
- A lateral way of relating—the way we relate to people who are next to us or who are our peers
- A downward way of relating—the way we relate to people who are under us

Those three types of relationships make for a healthy order in God's economy. By looking closer at each of these aligning relationships, we will understand more of the powerful effect of God's mighty hand upon our lives.

The people over you

God has appointed leaders in your life, under whose leadership you are to submit and let them be used in your life as God ordains. What does submission to those in authority really look like? How can we submit to our leaders, be a help to them, even be a delight to them—even when we disagree with their leadership?

If we talk about prophetic assignment as being at the right place, at the right time, with the right people, doing the right thing, we find ourselves sometimes being with the right people. They are people we know God has called to be leaders in our lives, who may, in fact, be doing a wrong thing that is working a right thing in us. God never told us that a leader would be placed in our lives who would always do the right thing.

On the contrary, the Bible is filled with examples of leaders who did not do the right thing. But God always used them. In the life of Saul, the things Saul did in the life of David were, for the most, wrong things. Yet God used them to produce right things in David. David was unwilling to respond in a manner that was unsubmissive and incorrect.

I can remember early on in my ministry as an associate pastor, when I served under a senior pastor who often was unfair and unkind with me. I went to the Lord, thinking,

Surely, Lord, You want me out of here. You are not going to allow this person to do these things or say these things.

And God said something that was very startling to me. He said, "Absolutely not! You stay right here. I am going to use this to work the very things in your life that I need to work." In that particular situation, as in other situations, God will say to you, "This is where I put you. You stay submitted... under the authority of this person, and I will use this in a powerful way in your life."

I had a sure word from the Lord that God was going to allow me to speak in all kinds of settings and groups, retreats, camps and so forth. That had been confirmed by others, and I thought, *Wow, I've got a prophetic assignment from the Lord.* But I was also living in proper alignment. So when these invitations began to come in, I went to my pastor and asked for his permission to go. Much to my surprise, he said to me, "No, you have plenty to do here at the church. There is no reason for you to go out and speak at these other places."

Initially it hurt me, and I didn't understand. But when I went back to God, God said, "You submit to the authority that is over you, but trust that what I have said, I have said." Many times since that time, God has opened to me door after door of ministry with opportunities to speak. But it was very important that I said yes to someone who was in authority over my life. That actually worked in me a deeper work of character preparing me for the days ahead when God opened up many more doors than I would have imagined.

All of us desire to have incredibly fair and loving leaders. We thank God for that, and we know that is the way God intends for leadership to be expressed and exhibited. But there are times when God will take the wrong things that people do to work the right things in our lives.

I found in my own life, as I submitted to something that I considered unfair and unjust, that God used it to work wonderful things in my life.

Elders and others in pastoral authority are a designated part of the mighty hand of God. If we resist divine authority, then our hearts become lifted up in pride. You and I cannot say whatever we want to say about leaders—spiritual or otherwise—and assume that God does not care about our words. You might be surprised to find Him resisting you—not because He thinks leaders are perfect, but because leaders are necessary and have been appointed by Him.

The people next to you

God has placed some interesting people next to you! As you move into proper alignment with God, it will be important for you to discover who is next to you spiritually—who your peers are in the Lord. God has brought some people into your life to help you live in accountability and to help sharpen you in your walk in the Lord.

One of the things that Paul said to Timothy was that he was to "run with the righteous, those who were pursuing God out of a pure heart." Timothy needed godly peers. People with whom he could live out his Christianity. Paul encouraged him to "flee youthly lusts, leave those things that were not of God and pursue God"—but not alone. He was to pursue God with those who were calling upon God from a pure heart. (See 1 Timothy 6:11; 2 Timothy 2:22.)

In my own life there is a number of pastors with whom I relate and walk. We challenge each other. In the church, I encourage our people to find others whom God has put in their life to run next to them. There is nothing better, whether you are riding a bike in the Tour de France or running a marathon—whatever the case may be—than to have someone who believes in you, who is there for you and who is helping you to ride or run at the best pace possible. That certainly is true in our spiritual life. God has called people to come alongside us. As Proverbs tells us, "As iron sharpens iron, so a man sharpens the countenance of his friend" (Prov. 27:17).

The people under you

This is where you find out who is under your spiritual influence—whether it's your children, teenagers in your youth group or somebody else younger than you in the Lord with whom God has given you influence.

I heard a great story recently about one of the volunteer workers in our children's ministry. She is a single woman who has no children. But God has called her into the children's ministry of our church. She was married early in her life, and that marriage ended. Through that she made a recommitment to Christ and has lived faithfully for the Lord for a number of years.

Not having children, she wondered what she could give to kids, but she really felt that God had called her to do that. She has been a part of the leadership for our children's ministry now for some time. She has been a very effective minister to the children. The kids call her "Miss Jen." One of the little girls in her class sat her mom down at home and wanted to play Sunday school. She was going to be Miss Jen, and her mom would be one of the children in the class. She took that opportunity to teach her mom about Jesus and all the things Miss Jen has taught her. The girl and her mom ran into Miss Jen at a store one day while shopping. The little girl ran to Miss Jen, threw her arms around Miss Jen's waist and told her how much she loved her and appreciated her ministry.

Whether it is a congregation that is under us, workers in a company or a preschool girl, that is part of living in proper alignment. Who knows what that little girl will become one day because of the investment that Miss Jen made in her life.

Another thing that we need to understand is that there are people who pretend to be submitted to leaders and, in fact, walk in what I would call "sweet rebellion." Sweet rebellion is an interesting concept because it has people who appear to be hearing everything you say and doing everything you do. But in fact, in their heart of hearts, they may be sitting down on the outside, but they are standing up on the inside. In their hearts, they are not in any way, shape or form submitting themselves to the authority of those who are over them. At some point you can count on the fact that for those who are not truly submitted but are walking in sweet rebellion, that rebellion will ultimately come to the surface, not only to the recognition of those who are in authority, but also will cause hurt and harm in the lives of those who are walking in sweet rebellion.

Servant Leaders

The relationships we have with people over us, next to us and under us are supernatural alignments that God has designed. These relationships teach us the importance of submission to authority, they provide us with camaraderie and they provide us with accountability through biblical friendships. They also teach us how to pour our lives into others as servant leaders.

In his letter to Christians scattered throughout the regions that Paul had evangelized on his mission trips, Peter advises the leaders reading his words to:

> Shepherd the flock of God which is among you, serving as overseers, not by compulsion but willingly, not for dishonest gain but eagerly; nor as being lords over those entrusted to you, but being examples to the flock.
>
> —1 Peter 5:2–3

Peter is saying, "Elders, this is what you do. Shepherd the flock of God, serving as overseers." *Shepherd*, *elder* and *overseer* are synonymous terms. They speak of one office—but of different functions of that office as a spiritual leader.

Either by reason of age or spiritual maturity, *elders* are older in the faith and are leaders whom God has put in authority over people's lives. As elders, they are to *shepherd* the people under them.

What does a shepherd do? A *shepherd* leads, feeds, guides and protects. Authority is a delegated gift from God to edify and empower another. One with spiritual authority over another is never to use that authority for personal good or gain—that authority is to be used only for the good of another person.

What do *overseers* do? Well, literally they oversee—or "see over." They look into your life and see what is happening in your life as you open the door for them to do that.

As servant leaders, we become God's delegated authority in the life of another. To lead successfully, as God intends, we will incorporate all three of these functions of a spiritual leader. God will not raise us to leadership until we are an "elder"—matured in our faith and ready to lead. As a leader we will "oversee" another's life, providing encouragement and help as God dictates. But it is only as we function as "shepherd" that we will be able to lead, feed, guide and protect those who have been placed under our spiritual authority.

Jesus Christ is our greatest example of a true servant leader. He led a collection of twelve rugged, impetuous, blue-collar fishermen to become the apostles of His early church. He fed the thousands—not just with five loaves and two fishes, but with spiritual food and drink that fully satisfied the hungry, thirsty hearts that pressed in close to Him. When the storms of life rushed over the lives of His followers, He guided them safely into the harbor of God's rest and calmly commanded the storm to be still. And He protected any who humbly placed themselves under His authority, wisely admonishing those who would harm another to look first at their own lives. "If you are without sin, go ahead and cast a stone at someone else," He counseled. Thus, as He protected, He still reached out to call others into humble submission to His Father.

Learn to be a servant who leads the way Jesus led. That's the way to be properly aligned with God and man. The greater the authority that you have, the greater the responsibility that you have to be the servant of all. That's what a servant leader does.

Watch Out for the "God-Told-Me" Card

As we live by prophetic assignment and in proper alignment, we must watch out for the appearance of the "God-told-me" trump card. Be careful of saying, "This is exactly what God told me to do, and this is exactly what I'm going to do!" when you are seeking to discern God's clear determination for what you are to do. By saying that, you have played the trump card. How can a wise counselor advise you otherwise? How can you open yourself to counsel with a closed approach like that? There must be clear balance between what we perceive to be a prophetic assignment and our position of proper alignment with those around us—and with God.

For example, a husband is the covering over his wife and family. But if he states arbitrarily, "This is what we are going to do, and this is how we are going to do it," then he has already negated any opportunity for his wife, his life's partner, to speak into the situation through her discernment from the Holy Spirit. And he has demeaned the input of wisdom that often arises "out of the mouths of babes."

As servant leaders, we become
God's delegated authority in the life of another.

The Bible clearly tells us, "Where there is no counsel, the people fall; but in the multitude of counselors there is safety" (Prov. 11:14). It is in the context of covenantal community that we see God communicate to us His plans and purposes for our lives. Living by prophetic assignment is never a mandate to live in *isolation.* Rather it is a mandate to live in the *insulation* that comes from being identified with God's people.

Does History Keep Repeating Itself in Your Life?

For some, it may feel as if nothing ever works out the way it should. Nothing ever goes quite right. Things take longer than they should take—and the end result is never quite what you imagined it to be. Yet, isn't the Christian life supposed to work? It is not supposed to be this way.

When this happens you may try to explain it away: "I just need to do more spiritual warfare." "I must be a real giant of faith for God to send this my way because a lesser person would have crumbled." But in fact, it may be that God is resisting you. And He may be resisting you because you are proud. Too proud to ask. Too proud to listen.

You may belong to the "new" generation—one that has maximized technology, science and intellect to get you through all of life's challenges. Or at least you think these things will get you through: When you get everything going just right, you will be awesome; all you need is a chance to show your stuff.

You will discover that the reason you have not been fully released into your calling is because there is a seed of rebellion against God's authority in your life. You do not really trust that God has your best interest at heart, so you try to take matters into your own hands. That's pride—lifting yourself above God.

Perhaps you don't even think about God at all. Maybe it never occurred to you that God can speak—to you.

Or you may just believe that you have lived life long enough to know just how to make it work—*alone*—without God or anybody else. Like a famous Frank Sinatra song, you say, "I'll do it my way." But why doesn't your way seem to work anymore?

Again, the problem with pride is that it lifts you up and brings God down—which ultimately makes you God. If you are in charge, then you are God. You lift yourself up to the level of God when you assert, "I'm going to do whatever I want, and this and that is going to happen."

Either you are going to let God be God, or you are going to be God. And if you want to be God, then again, I promise you, it will not go well for you. Remember that Saul lost his kingdom. Worse even than that, in the New Testament Ananias and Sapphira lost their lives! (See Acts 5.)

But deciding to lift God—rather than yourself—to a place of preeminent prominence in your life is a decision you must make. Some of us are pretty tough when it comes to facing up to the will of God for our lives. Like Jonah, even while sitting in the belly of the fish—where life is stinky, dark and crummy—we would rather not repent and obey God's call. As a result, we continue facing the same tests, without moving forward.

You may have kicked against the Lord's dealings for a long time. Believe it or not, you are in good company. We all have involved ourselves in that same resistance at one time or another.

As a matter of fact, the great missionary Saul of Tarsus—we know him as the apostle Paul—kicked against God's purposes for years. Finally, Jesus Himself appeared to him on the road to Damascus and asked him, "Saul, why are you persecuting Me?" That dramatic encounter brought Paul to his knees in humility and repentance. And from that place, Paul found grace and favor from the Lord despite being a former persecutor of the church.

But, like Paul, some people go down hard, resisting God every step of the way. This is so unnecessary. Don't you want to be somebody who doesn't have to go down the hard way? God does not want us to be people who learn everything the hard way. He wants us to be people who learn from Him. He wants us to be people who willingly humble ourselves under His mighty hand. Which way would you rather learn: by going through the School of Hard Knocks, where the school colors are black and blue and most of us fail the tests, or by going through the School of the Spirit, where we letter in peace and joy and graduate with a ring that says, "God is for *me!*"

The simple fact of our resisting God is this: If history continues to repeat itself in your life, then there is only one constant factor in each situation you encounter: you! If you keep coming around to the same mountain time and time again, I think it is safe to say that it is *you*—and not God—causing these same results time and time again.

When you feel the mighty hand of God working something out of you and into you, do not resist it. As you come under God's hand, you will be shaped and formed so that you can be lifted up. Whatever God has promised you, He will fulfill it as long as you keep yourself under His mighty hand.

You need to learn the fact that when people occupy positions of spiritual authority, sometimes others get hurt. That is an unfortunate truth. But again, in God's plan, there is no Plan B. It is impossible for us to say we are just going to be under God's authority and not under the authority of any man. It simply will not work that way.

Obviously, however, you should not submit to any authority who would tell you to do something immoral or illegal. Authority figures are not always right. Leaders have to earn the trust of those in submission to them, and every leader should make sure he or she is in leadership for the right reason.

Part of growing up in the Lord means gaining this understanding—that we are to be "subject one to another" in humility because none of us are perfect yet. Let's face it: All of us have feet of clay. We all share the "common cup of humanity." I have feet of clay, and I make mistakes. I disappoint people. I do things for which I have to apologize.

All of us will experience, either as leaders or followers, hurt and rejection in our lives. There will be plenty of opportunities where we were wrong or will be wrong, and we will need to repent and be forgiven and go on. There are other times when there will be things done to us or said about us that are just plain wrong. That happened in my life. I thought that as those things were happening, I was forgiving and letting them go. But God revealed to me that I wasn't. I had no idea that I held anger in my heart toward certain people who over the years had rejected me or hurt me in some way. I had no idea that a seed of anger had been sown in my heart.

Specifically, there were people who had misrepresented and mischaracterized me and my character, actions and motives. I don't claim to be someone who is perfect with regard to the facts or the truth in every situation, but I would say that I have a great love for the truth. I try very hard to represent people accurately and find it extremely distasteful when people slander or mischaracterize another person. In this case, it was me. While I had said the words, "I forgive," there was still something I was hanging on to, waiting for God to finish what He had to do in these people's lives.

If history continues to repeat itself in your life, then there is only one constant factor in each situation you encounter: you!

I had to learn a very important lesson from the Lord about what it really meant to let those things go. When I came under God's mighty hand, He exposed my heart and showed me something ugly in my life. He wanted it out of me. He was not interested in seeing me try to prove other people wrong. I needed to repent, forgive and release. He wanted me to glorify Him and allow Him to deal with the other people in His own way.

You may be on the Potter's wheel. God wants to shape you for the day when He lifts you up at the right time. Just stay under His hand. You may feel the thumb of the Lord as He presses you while molding and shaping you. Don't jump off the wheel, and don't try to take matters into your own hands.

What you are going through right now might be painful. God might be showing you things that you never knew you would have to deal with in your life; you might be discovering attitudes in your heart that you never knew were there. But the mighty hand of God is shaping you so He can release you in due time to the thing to which He has called you.

There was a recent season in my life where God granted, by His hand, some real promotion and some real fruitful ministry success, the likes of which would cause people to sit up and take notice. They would maybe say some really kind, positive things. All that is fine. But one of the lessons I learned in that is whenever people are commenting on God's hand of promotion in your life, because it is truly God's hand of promotion, we are never to internalize that and let that become part of us as though we were the ones who made any of that happen.

God is the source. We are the channels. We are the instruments, the earthen vessels. But the treasure and the glory is of Him. We are never to touch the glory and take any of that for ourselves. For me, it was subtle, and in a certain way I was impervious to and unaware of what was taking place in my heart. Suffice it to say that I just began to believe a little bit of my own press. I began to let a seed of pride be planted in my heart.

As with most of us, the root of that was twofold: First, trying to overcome insecurities by feeling secure in the work that we are doing, rather than finding the fullness of our security in who we are in Christ. The second part was tied to having experienced some criticism and rejection over the years, and maybe having a bit of an attitude that said, "See, I told you that these kind of things were going to happen in my life."

What I began to experience was the mighty hand of God that had promoted me now was beginning to resist me and to reveal to me the issues in the heart that had to be weeded out if I was going to be able to move on and find the fullness of what God wanted to do in my life. It was painful, but it was necessary. I repented of it privately with people with whom I work and publicly before the congregation. I felt the same hand that had promoted me then resisted me, and then began to promote me again. I do not want to forget that season or time, because I don't ever want to go back to that place. I want to see God do whatever He wants to do in my life. I want Him to receive the honor and glory and for my life always to be a sign and a wonder that point to Him—never to me.

I would say to anyone else: When God's hand begins to resist you and begins to reveal things to you, don't resist God's hand. Many believers will feel the resistance of God and call it the devil. Never call discipline demonic. We must learn to discern between the divine and the demonic. The demonic will always seek either to puff us up or to tear us down and destroy us. The divine will always open us up and reveal to us areas of sin so that we can confess, repent, be reconciled to God and restored to the place that He wants us to be. Then we can move on to greater and greater levels of His grace and glory in our lives, always remembering that it is by His grace, and it is to Him that we give the glory.

Humble yourself under the mighty hand of God, and He will lift you up. But if you allow your heart to be lifted up, the same hand that promoted you then resists you. If you repent and get humble again, then His hand will once again come under you and lift you up. I am profoundly grateful that we serve the God of the second chance—and the third and fourth chance, too, for that matter!

Lordship vs. Discipleship

One of the hindrances to our being in proper alignment is living like a lord rather than as a disciple.

Lords assert; disciples ask. Disciples say, "Lord, what do You want me to do?"—and then do whatever the Lord requires of them.

God has called us as His disciples to be servants. Servants do not walk around their master's house saying to one another, "You know what I'm going to do this year? I'm going to redecorate the library. And all this stuff is coming down. We're putting up a splash of color here, a splash of color there."

What if the master who owns the house were to hear that? What do you think he would have to say about it?

"I heard you and the other servant talking in here. What were you talking about?"

"Oh, master, we're going to redecorate the whole place."

"Are you really? Don't you realize this is not *your* home?

Don't you know that this is *my* place?"

Perhaps it is easier to look at a particular local church and say, "Yes, that's what is happening there. They are changing everything according to their desires and the desires and demands of their people. They just don't care what God wants anymore, only what they want."

Now obviously this is a danger for any church. There is no particular way of doing things—provided that it does not disobey a direct command of Scripture that is necessarily right or wrong. But we need to be careful that as church leaders, we don't say, "This year, this is what we are going to do . . . are going to change this." "We are going to have this program." "I just read this book on this particular thing, and this is what I'm going to do." That is one of the big mistakes many ministers made in the eighties during the age of the church growth movement. It was more about a consumeristic strategy than it was a prophetic assignment from God concerning their ministry. It's true, we got people in the doors. But they often left as quickly as they came.

Whatever you are doing in your church, the question that needs to be answered is, "Is this something that we believe God has called us to do? Have we prayed through in the presence of many witnesses, leaders in our church and sought wise counsel?" Can we say, as they did at the Jerusalem counsel, "It seemed good to us and to the Holy Spirit to do these particular things"? That is the integration of prophetic assignment and proper alignment—wanting what God wants and discovering what God wants in the context of prayer, fasting and wise counsel of those over you, next to you and under you.

But the same desire to assert rather than to ask takes place over and over again in our own personal lives. We can "redecorate the temple" without even considering that we are not our own. We belong to God—we are His temple.

I remember a man that was a part of our church in Southern California. He was forever making major changes in his life without considering if it was God or not. He went from business to business to business. Anything that sounded good to him, felt good to him, seemed to hold out the promise of being able to do well and make large sums of money was what he went after. The results in his life were disastrous. He went from one failure to another.

He was not a man without intelligence or talent or drive. This was a man without a sure word from God. In the end, his wife and children became very discouraged and lost respect for him and confidence in him.

What we are talking about here is of major importance to all of us in our lives. Whether or not we can use our skills for a while and be successful or whether we go from failure to failure, the point is that God always has a better plan than we do. We must walk in a way that is always seeking Him for what that plan and purpose is.

There is an elder in our church, a man who is very gifted in the area of business. But he has really latched on to this concept of living by prophetic assignment and in proper alignment. I have watched him make moves in business that just did not make sense from what you would typically think of as sound business practices. I have watched him start a business to help out another brother who was also starting a business, simply because God told him to do that. I have watched this man send customers to other companies because he felt other companies had a better product than he had to offer. When it seemed that he could strike the "big deal," I have seen him take time to mentor a young man in business because God instructed him to take this young man under his wing.

I have also watched as God has continued to find 101 different ways to bless this man financially. He truly is an example of one who has been blessed and is a blessing to others. Now he is teaching other businessmen how to make sure that they walk in God's kingdom agenda rather than their own.

True servants ask their master, "Sir, what would you have me to do?"

The good news for us is that even though we are under God our Master, He treats us like sons and daughters who have a full inheritance in everything He has when we submit to Him as Lord. We get to share in everything that our Master has at His table.

We get to share in our heavenly Father's miraculous and overwhelming inheritance. But to do so, we must humble ourselves under His mighty hand. Submission, without which proper alignment cannot occur, is to God first and then to His delegated authority. It is our pathway to promotion.

In Your Hands

My future's in Your hands,
My destiny secure.
I'll cease from all my striving
For Your way is strong and sure.
For all of my tomorrows
As with my yesterdays,
I'll trust Your hand to lift me up
And keep me by Your grace.

—Lyrics by Dale Evrist

Chapter 4

A Hand of Promotion

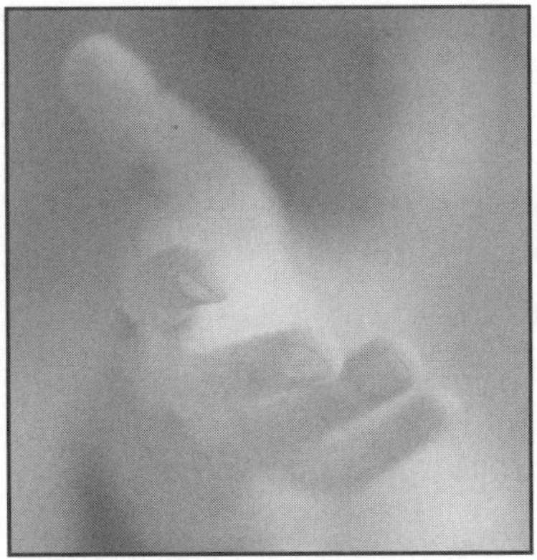

Sue left my office depressed, discouraged and a little angry. After spending four years doing a short radio spot on Christian radio, she had attended the National Religious Broadcasters Convention where she submitted a demo tape of a proposed television version of the spots dealing with marriage and family issues. She had received a very positive response at the convention to her work, but for some reason she didn't feel complete peace about airing the spots on television at that time.

Sue sought the input of her husband, and then she came to see me. When Sue and I met, I had affirmed the call of God that was on her life and my belief that God was going to use her in significant ways in the months and years ahead.

Yet I also felt that God was taking Sue into a season of being hidden by God from public ministry. He was taking her into a time of private ministry in which her primary calling was to minister to her husband and her children. During this season God was giving her husband a much larger public profile, and her ministry helped him make this transition.

I also shared my belief that if she stayed in the center of God's will and God's timing, her whole household would prosper. I shared that God would release her in due time, and when He did, that to which He released her would be better and stronger than what she had known before.

Yet it seemed as if a heavy cloud of disappointment and grief hung over her for a number of days after our meeting. She knew God was setting her aside from public view for a season. She loved her husband and children and was committed to doing whatever she needed to do for them. But it was still difficult for her to lay down something that she loved, that she was good at and that for which she seemed to be getting greater opportunities.

It was not until she phoned the television stations and told them that she was not ready to air the television program she had proposed that the cloud lifted.

A few months later, she laid down her radio ministry, too—submitting it to God while trusting that He would raise it back up again in His timing. Most importantly, though, she knew she was obeying God when she did this.

As Sue humbled herself under the mighty hand of God, indeed she did experience a season of being hidden. But what at first seemed strange and uncomfortable to her gave way to a season of sweet solitude that led to a greater intimacy in her relationship with the Lord and to her being able to serve her husband and her growing family well.

God promoted her husband in a very wonderful and supernatural way. In the beginning of this experience, while she was seeing her husband being lifted up and promoted—which was a great joy to her—she still questioned if God would ever use her again. In some ways it felt as if God had completely passed her over. But she continued to remind herself about the promises of God and continued to trust God to lift her up at the right time.

After two years Sue had learned to trust God and serve Him selflessly. She had found contentment and joy in being His daughter and no longer needed the recognition that she had thought. She needed only His recognition and the love of those whom God had put in her life.

At that time God awakened in Sue a sense that His hand of promotion was about to lift her up in the near future. As that was happening in Sue's heart, in my heart God began to make me aware that He had placed an anointing upon Sue in the area of education and training. God permitted me to be used as an instrument to release Sue to become the pastor of education at New Song.

She now directs our LIFE School of Ministry, which is a college-level training school. She also oversees our New Song Christian Academy, grades K–12.

As God's hand of promotion has lifted her up, Sue has felt His peace and His protection. When she sought man's hand of promotion—or her own hand of promotion—she experienced a level of fear and insecurity. As she has learned to come completely under God's mighty hand, she not only is confident that God is using her in the position that she holds today, but she also knows she can trust Him for other things that He will lift her up to in the future.

Great News: God Has Great Things for You

If there is one thing we can learn from Sue's life, it is that God says to all of us, "If you come under My hand, I will exalt you in due time. I will put you in a place where your works will have eternal value. You will make a difference in people's lives. I will even reverse the power of those things that used to thwart you, and they will become a blessing to you."

That is precisely what God did in Sue's life. God took from her the very thing she thought she needed most in life: recognition from others. He showed her the greater blessing of receiving her recognition from Him. Then He re-released her into a place of public, fruitful ministry.

When God's blessing becomes my achievement I have opened a very dangerous door—one that can lead me into pride.

In the process, she learned she did not need to be afraid of God or man. And she learned that she did not need to promote herself. She let go and let God do it.

As a Christian you are part of the Abrahamic covenant. Part of what that means is that the desire you have in your heart for significance is legitimate. That desire for significance was given to you by God. It is part of our inheritance as the spiritual children of Abraham. God said to Abraham, "I will bless you and make your name great" (Gen. 12:2).

Sue wanted to be a blessing. She wanted to have an impact, to make a difference.

It is a righteous thing to want to be part of something significant—even to want your name to be attached to it. That is not wrong, provided that we find our primary significance in our relationship with God and who we are in Christ.

But we run into problems when we get attached to the thing itself—what we view as being significant. When a blessing from God begins to be "my talent," "my ministry," "my accomplishment," it will cease to satisfy us. When *God's blessing* becomes *my achievement* I have opened a very dangerous door—one that can lead me into pride.

Living in a college town, I have the privilege of interacting with college students who are pursuing various degrees. In a very real sense the process of education is not about a degree. It is, in fact, about learning to trust God to a greater degree.

Yet how many college students have I seen who, when they come to that time of graduation and commencement, will put too much emphasis on the fact of that achievement and the earning of the degree and not upon the blessing of God walking them through that four-year or more journey. Most of them I have seen will quickly realize that the achievement will ring very hollow in their heart if it is not tied to the blessing of walking with God through the process. And there must be evidence that they have finished one aspect of their journey, and the door is opening to another. They must learn how to embrace and enjoy the journey they are on with the Lord.

You may think that God could never do great things with you. But that also can be a form of pride that comes from thinking that you know more than God. God desires that each of us makes a significant contribution to advance His kingdom. To be ready to do that, we simply submit to Him. Then we simply follow Him in the calling He gives to us.

Eternity will show the significance of the role that we play in the kingdom of God.

When you say things like, "*I* can" or "*I* should" or "*I* can't," those statements center on *you* rather than on God. In that sense, such a statement becomes an expression of pride.

What we need to say is, "I'm coming under God, and I am going to trust God that whatever He wants to do with me, wherever He wants to put me, that's what I'll do and that's where I'll go. If He wants to make me a history-maker where my name is written in books, then fine. If He wants to make me a nameless, faceless person, serving in obscurity, then that's fine—because I know that when I'm serving Him it isn't obscurity in His eyes." Eternity will show the significance of the role that we play in the kingdom of God.

Promotion: Man's Hand vs. God's Hand

What do you think when you hear the word *promotion*? More

money? More self-respect? A new house? A new car?

If you have ever had such thoughts, then you are probably typical of most people who want an upwardly mobile lifestyle. Most of us think about promotion as it relates to our career or our status in society.

If, for example, a really nice promotion were to come to us—let's say, a job promotion—most of us would be flying high for a while, probably thinking our lives were better because of this new opportunity.

No doubt we would want to "work" the good news for a while. Maybe we would tell people how that dream house we have had our eye on is about to become a reality, or how we finally got the recognition we deserved for all our hard work, or how the kids could now go to private school—or any number of other things.

That kind of reaction is pretty normal. Being promoted can be exciting. There isn't anything wrong with wanting to tell others about something exciting that has happened to us.

But promotion—whether career or otherwise—can have a way of inflating our pride. The feeling of personal success that a promotion brings can make it easy for us to think we are doing pretty well—based on our own efforts. It can cause us to stop depending upon God's hand to promote us. Soon we believe in our own abilities to such an extent that we start to believe our way is the best way to get ahead in life.

Not so.

True, we can go places in life by working hard, doing a good job, making the right contacts, not giving up and so on. After all, hard work does pay off, sometimes resulting in success or recognition.

But as Christians we need to understand that our reliance on self-effort is not God's pathway to promotion. We know from the Bible that God's kind of promotion does not come primarily from us or from other people. *It comes from Him:*

> I said to the boastful, "Do not deal boastfully," and to the

> wicked, "Do not lift up the horn. Do not lift up your horn on high; do not speak with a stiff neck." For exaltation comes neither from the east nor from the west nor from the south. But God is the Judge: He puts down one, and exalts another... "All the horns of the wicked I will also cut off, but the horns of the righteous shall be exalted."
>
> —PSALM 75:4–7, 10

These verses speak of true promotion—the kind that's life-giving and lasting. And they tell us that true promotion comes from God.

Promotion is "the act or fact of being raised in position or rank; the act of furthering the growth or development of something." That's pretty simple stuff. It says plainly enough what promotion is.

But it says nothing about how promotion is accomplished from a biblical perspective.

In 1 Peter 5:6, God's Word tells us clearly how promotion happens: If you come under the mighty hand of God, then the mighty hand of God comes under you—and lifts you up. In that verse we read, "Therefore humble yourselves under the mighty hand of God, that He may exalt you in due time."

Always remember that the greatest work God does through us will be the work He does in us.

When the Bible refers to the hand of God it is usually referring to His power and ability. So coming under the hand of God means depending on God's power and ability first, last and always—and not on our own.

Therefore, with God promotion is more about *how* than *what.* The how of promotion is critical to Him and may even be more important than the *what* to which He promotes us.

Always remember that the greatest work God does through us will be the work He does in us. Humble yourself under the mighty hand of God and get promoted. It's just that simple.

Why? Because God is for you. God loves you. God has plans and purposes for your life that He wants to accomplish. If we are proud, we thwart those purposes because God resists us. If we are humble, we advance those purposes because it is God who advances us.

We need to get an entirely different perspective on life. We need to learn to keep the main thing the main thing. And the main thing is always *ministry*. It is always about serving. Any place to which God promotes us is always about giving us a greater sphere and a greater opportunity to serve more people.

A person in business needs this perspective. Instead of the mind-set that insists, "Sell hard and close the sale," the Christian businessman and businesswoman will think, *How can I make this sale the best deal for my client?*

Let's say you are a real estate agent. Why would you want to press hard to sell a home to someone if in fact that home may not even be the one they need? Your job, as a Christian, is not as much to sell homes as it is to help a person find a home that best suits their family and their budget.

If you are a store owner, then ultimately your job is not to get people to buy your products. Your job is to serve every person who comes through your door and make sure they walk out with what they need—not what you can sell them.

I know a member of our church who is an extremely gifted salesman with lots and lots of years of experience. Once when he was selling insurance packages, a potential client began to describe the kind of insurance package he needed. As the client described his needs, the salesman realized that although he had a package somewhat similar to what the client needed, a competing company had the exact insurance package the man was looking for. So rather than trying to sell his client his package, he referred him to the other company.

The client was stunned and asked, "Why would you send me to a competitor?"

This opened the door for him to answer, "Well, I'm a Christian businessman, and my job really is not as much to sell insurance as it is to make sure I serve everyone who comes through my door."

His client went to the other company and got the insurance package he needed. But as a result, God blessed our church member even more in his business—and continues to prosper him to this day.

Humble yourself under the mighty hand of God and get promoted. It's just that simple.

That's the way the kingdom works: Humble yourself, get promoted.

> Give, and it will be given to you: good measure, pressed down, shaken together, and running over will be put into your bosom. For with the same measure that you use, it will be measured back to you.
>
> —Luke 6:38

This principle is reminiscent of the classic movie *Miracle on 34th Street*, where Kris Kringle (Edmund Gwenn)—the Macy's store Santa—began to send customers to the competing department store because it had the very thing these people were looking for and Macy's didn't. Initially, management was up in arms. Someone asked, "Why in the world would anyone from Macy's send someone to another department store?"

Yet more and more people began to shop at Macy's. Any store that would care enough about its customers to send them to a competing store to find the right product was the kind of store these people wanted to shop in. That's a kingdom principle that will work in every area of life.

Let's say you are a car salesman, and you know whether or not the warranty your boss is telling you to sell is really worthwhile—an item a car buyer really needs. If it isn't worthwhile, do not sell it. If you do, you are defrauding your customer.

Instead, watch God promote you and make you salesman of the month, salesman of the quarter, salesman of the year perhaps. Your boss will say, "I don't understand it. You don't do things the way the other salesmen do, and yet you continue to sell and sell." When that happens, you have an opportunity to give glory to the God who promoted you.

God will lift you up and prosper you if you make serving and ministering to people your goal. In that way your life becomes a sign and a wonder—a story of His glory. When people ask why you do things in an unorthodox way—a way that is not "business as usual"—tell them, "It may not be *secular* business as usual, but it is *kingdom* business as usual." You can therefore point people to the King and His kingdom.

Some large companies have a full-time position called "director of promotions." Often this position is reserved for those individuals who can promote or publicize the company's achievements, reputation or new enterprises in such a way that the company receives the benefits of greater recognition, new investment money or wider appreciation for its reputation.

In the entertainment industry especially, men and women in the promotional field work very hard to promote, publicize or draw favor for their clients—who may include movie stars, singers, entertainers or other kinds of celebrities. A significant amount of money may be spent on a publicity campaign to focus as much national or international attention on the client as possible.

Expensive press materials, capital for radio, video or television spots, aggressive requests for newspaper and magazine interviews, premiers, autograph signings, promotional tours and many other elements of creating publicity are employed for the sole purpose of focusing as much attention as possible on the one who benefits from being seen or heard. When that happens successfully, everyone up and down the line who helped promote that person reaps more financial rewards.

However, from heaven's side of things, this way of living by "making something of ourselves" actually can result in making nothing of ourselves in the end. It was Jesus who said, "If you, on your own, try to find your life, you'll lose it; you'll miss it. But if you'll lose your life for My sake, then you'll find life that is life indeed." (See Matthew 10:39.)

Let me hasten to say that none of these things, in and of themselves, are immoral, improper or unbiblical. We simply need to be very, very careful that, again, the goal of everything we do is ministry—not money. Our strategy in promotion is working hand in hand with God's hand in lifting something up that is worthwhile and that will help many, many people. This can be very tricky at times, provided that everyone in the process remains humbled before the Lord, seeking God's face and holding one another accountable. This is the essence of prophetic assignment and proper alignment. Then we can do publicity God's way.

A wonderful example of this in the Scripture would be John the Baptist. He was Jesus' "front man," if you will. He announced to everyone that there was someone coming after him they needed to hear, heed and respond to. That was a wonderful example of God-ordained publicity that paved the way for the ministry that was to follow. There is definitely a right way to do it. We must make sure we are giving ourselves to the spirit of the kingdom and not to the spirit of the world.

From the world's side of things, it looks as if a person has really made something of himself. I suppose that from the world's standpoint, you could say that is true—but we are not of this world. We have to be very careful not to allow worldly principles to crowd out kingdom principles in our lives. There is a reason why we call God's kingdom the "upside-down kingdom." It is radically different from the way the world does things.

Jesus instructed us to be "wise as serpents and harmless as doves" (Matt. 10:16). We can be wise as serpents in the way we use the world's resources. But we must also be as harmless as doves. As true disciples of the Lord Jesus Christ who are following His kingdom principles, we are aware that what seems upside down to the world is really right side up from heaven's perspective.

We are not trying to be self-made men and women. We are allowing ourselves to be made by God's hand into the image of our Lord and Savior Jesus Christ. Christ's whole life was about submission to His heavenly Father, about serving and giving His life away for people in every way possible—even to the point of death on the cross. What looked like an absolute humiliation and defeat at Calvary turned out to be the greatest triumph and greatest gift that anyone had ever given.

We do not want our lives to be a testimony to our own abilities because that will get us nothing in heaven. That testimony will not last for eternity. Some of the wealthiest people in the world enter into eternity absolutely bankrupt and empty-handed. It is true they made a lot of money. But what does that really accomplish? And what kind of legacy is that, really? All they have to show for their lives is the wealth they accumulated, and yet they did not take a penny of it with them.

Let's say that you are successful in business or politics. If it is not done for God and by God's plan and purpose, then what does that *really* accomplish, and how does it really matter? Maybe you think what you are doing is far superior in significance to what your fellow man is doing when you stack your achievements next to his. Well, maybe your accomplishments *are* significant when you compare them that way.

But in James 4:14 we read:

> You do not know what will happen tomorrow. For what is your life? It is even a vapor that appears for a little time and then vanishes away.

God is saying that the sum of our lives compared with the significance of eternity is like our breath on a cold day. It appears as a vapor for a second or two, and then it is gone for good. We're just here for a short while, and then we vanish away. We *must* make sure that we are living the life that we were born to live.

Know Who Is Promoting You

It is important for us to determine who is lifting us up—our own hand, someone else's hand or the mighty hand of God.

For that reason, I am concerned about the concept we know as *promotion* and with the function of *promoters*. Again, let me be clear in stating that I do not have a problem with it if we see promoters as advocates for someone whom God's hand is really upon. "Promotion" that attempts to inform as many people as possible about a wonderful ministry opportunity, a wonderful product that will help them or a wonderful talent or gift that will bless them works for me. I'm OK with promotion for those reasons.

In the same way, we need to exercise caution when it comes to the matter of people in a certain walk of life who require a manager or are a manager. One can define management as trying to "sell" another person. But Christian managers should define management as saying, "I believe God's hand is on this person, and I want to help other people know about this person. I believe that as a manager I'm cooperating with God's plan and purpose for my life and for this person's life."

If that is what we are after, then we will be fine. A manager or anyone who is representing another person is supposed to play the role of an advocate. That is what a manager is meant to be. A true manager will understand *Holy Spirit-inspired advocacy.*

Holy Spirit-inspired advocacy happens when you see God's hand on someone and you know that He has given you the call to be a channel to get that person to a place where they can touch many more people. You—as well as that person—are saying, "Yes, I believe this is what God has called me to."

Even if this is the case, we still have to exercise caution. As human beings we are very capable of self-promotion. But rather than promoting self, we must be cooperating with God's promotion. I know this can sound like semantics. But it really isn't.

To be men and women of God who are submitted to Him and confident that His hand is on us and under us, we will ask ourselves very challenging questions. There are many kinds of things that we *could do*—but they aren't necessarily what we should do. Just because we *can* does not mean we *should.*

We must continually bring under God's will the sum of both our lives and the people's lives that we represent or touch. We must make sure that we are submitted to God and that God is the one who is doing the promoting.

Make no mistake about it: Man can promote; that is for sure. But which would you rather have promoting you—the feeble hand of man apart from God, which at some point will ultimately fail, or the mighty hand of God strengthening the hand of man promoting you, which never fails?

Combating the "Star Mentality"

The idea of "Christian celebrity" is something I feel strongly about. The acceptance of Christian music artists, authors, sports figures, entertainers or politicians as stars really, at some level, becomes a form of idolatry. To me the whole star and celebrity mentality—the way we worship celebrities—is a bizarre thing. Simply because somebody can run with a football, act or exercise a particular talent, people tend to idolize them and believe those individuals to be more special than other people.

By setting people up as stars and looking at them that way we tend to wind up focusing more on man than on God. It is always a dangerous thing when we lose sight of God being the One who ultimately gives each person the talent to do what he or she is able to do. When that happens, our inclination is to praise people. But we must always remember that the praise belongs to God.

Now at this point you may be asking, "But Dale, isn't there a principle of giving honor to whom honor is due? Doesn't the

Bible say, 'Let another man's lips praise you and not your own'? So why would the Bible give us room to praise and honor people if we weren't allowed to do it?"

Just because we can does not mean we should.

Please let me make this clear. I am not saying that we cannot honor people, and I am not saying that we cannot praise people. But what we honor is their obedience to allow God to use them in the gifts that He has given them in a way that brings honor to them. When we praise them and thank them, there is nothing wrong with saying, "What you did was wonderful," provided that we understand that we are always honoring the Giver of those gifts. More than anything, what we are praising and honoring in another person is the way they have, in a wise and godly fashion, stewarded those gifts and released them in a way that brings praise to God and joy and ministry to the hearts of people.

We want to always have a clear view of the hand of God promoting us. We should be in awe of the work of God in people's lives—whatever they are doing. But we cannot do that if we confuse talent with calling or with faithfulness.

I am reminded of a story in Charles M. Sheldon's book *In His Steps* where a fabulously gifted opera singer chose to give her life to singing in a rescue mission for outcasts and derelicts. She had dared to ask the question, "What would Jesus do?" She believed that singing in the rescue mission was the way God wanted her to use her talent. People who want to do only what God calls them to simply say yes to God.

Be that kind of a person. Look only to God for promotion. Step out with your talents and gifts only in the places God calls you to step. Make your life a song of praise to God—giving all the glory to Him. Get fully under the mighty hand of God. When you do, God will promote you because you are ready to be promoted.

Your Hands

Your hands,
Your hands
Hold the seasons and the signs.
Your hands,
Your hands
Hold these hopes and dreams of mine.
Your hands,
Your hands
Hold my purpose and my time.
So I humbly place my life
In Your hands.

Lyrics by Dale Evrist

Chapter 5

When God's Hand of Promotion Lifts You Up

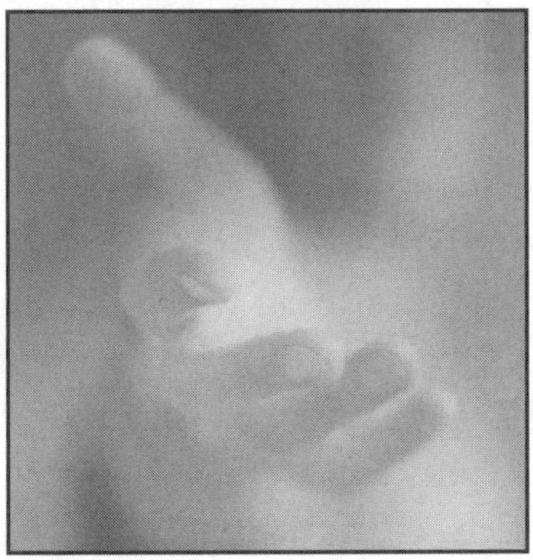

If God's promises to promote you have not been fulfilled in your life yet, it is because you are not ready for them to be fulfilled. But as long as you walk humbly with God and stay submitted to Him, then He will lift you up and accomplish those promises in His timing.

If you will choose to believe this—if you can really grab hold of it—then it will save you much grief in your walk with God and release great blessings in your walk with Him.

Remember, if there is a place—whether a ministry, a location, a vision—that you believe God has called you to, and you are not there yet, then it is because you are not ready to be there yet.

But don't lose heart. Just continue to walk humbly with God and you will be there in due time. When you understand that being humbled under the mighty hand of God is the safest, most secure position you can be in, then God will work things out of you, and He will work things into you.

Right Place, Right Time, Right People, Right Things

What does it look like when you are living under the mighty hand of God—in prophetic assignment and proper alignment? He will lift you up and put you in place so that you will be where He wants you to be, doing what He wants you to do and fulfilling His plan at the time He wants you to be doing it. You will be in the right place at the right time with the right people, doing the right things.

That is such a merciful thing for God to do with us. Even if our promotion comes later than we would like it to, it is going to happen if we live in submission to the mighty hand of God. That's because His way is the way of increase. Things always get bigger as God continues to change us from glory to glory. And remember, often when the reaping is later—it is greater.

John the Baptist knew what it was to wait on the fulfillment of God's promises for his life. He served God in obscurity while he waited for the Lord to do what He said He would do. John's father, Zacharias, prophesied over John as an infant, saying he would become the "prophet of the Most High." He did—but not until *years* after his father's prophecy.

> And you, child, will be called the prophet of Highest; for you will go before the face of the Lord to prepare His ways; to give knowledge of salvation to His people by the remission of their sins, through the tender mercy of our God, with which the Dayspring from on high has visited us; to give light to those who sit in darkness and the shadow of death, to guide our feet into the way of peace.
>
> —Luke 1:76–79

Obviously this prophecy could not have been fulfilled while

John was an infant. But the scriptural accounts of John the Baptist show that the fulfillment of the promise happened only when God was ready for it to happen. And when He was ready, He called John by the Holy Spirit out of the wilderness and promoted him publicly before all of Israel:

> So the child grew and became strong in spirit, and was in the deserts till the day of his manifestation to Israel.
>
> —Luke 1:80

Think for a minute what this calling meant for John. He lived for years in the wilderness—praying, eating weird food, wearing strange clothes, waiting on God and being prepared by God. Talk about staying submitted under the mighty hand of God!

Remember, often when the reaping is later—it is greater.

And when God did promote him, He gave him a platform only for a short time. His flame burned brightly, but briefly. Crowds came from everywhere to hear John preach and to see his ministry. Then one day God said to him, "John, there—coming toward you—that's the Lamb of God who takes away the sins of the entire world. Your profile is decreasing now. His has to increase. You have to step down because He needs to step up. The people need to start hearing Him now instead of you."

So after years of living in the desert, God allowed John to serve only a matter of months in his calling. Then he submitted himself under the mighty hand of God in a new way. He had to decrease—to fade from the scene.

First, John was put in prison. Now, do you think John sat in his cell saying, "Well, isn't this nice. Thank You very much, God. I gave my whole life to You, and You only let me minister for a few months. You even allow me to be thrown in prison." That was not John's attitude. It's true, he did face discouragement and doubt after his arrest, wondering if Jesus really was the One who had been promised or whether he should look for another. But he ultimately settled this issue in his heart, and Jesus had this to say about him:

> Assuredly, I say to you, among those born of women there has not risen one greater than John the Baptist.
>
> —Matthew 11:11

John the Baptist was a voice that was heard only for a short time because that is what God had planned for him. But John the Baptist accomplished more in that number of months than many people do in their entire lifetime, so much so that Jesus referred to John the Baptist, his ministry and his life as something great.

Would it be OK to you for God to take His time with you and release you *later* rather than *sooner* in order to do something great in your life?

If God Lifts Us Up, He Will Keep Us Up

If God's hand lifts us up, it will keep us up for as long as it takes for us to fulfill God's assignment and calling in our lives.

God wants to promote us because He loves us. Yes, we have made mistakes and failed God so many times. We have let our hearts be lifted up, and we have been proud at times in our lives. God gave us opportunities, and we blew them.

But we serve a God of great mercy and great grace. We need to understand that God's will for our lives is a narrow path, but His grace is a broad plain.

The Bible is filled with the evidence of God's grace. In Romans 5:20 we read:

> The Ten Commandments were given so that all could see the extent of their failure to obey God's laws. But the more we see our sinfulness, the more we see God's abounding grace forgiving us.
>
> —TLB

Even greater than *reading what God says* about His grace is *seeing how God responds* when His people fail to live according to His will. God's Word is filled with stories about great men and women of God who failed Him at one point in their lives and really needed His grace—and He gave it freely! Noah, Abraham and David needed forgiving grace—and got it. Ruth, a woman from the heathen country of Moab, Rahab, the prostitute, and Bathsheba, the adulteress, became the grandmothers of Jesus. Peter denied his relationship to Jesus three times, yet he became a great apostle of the early church.

We need to understand that God's will for our lives is a narrow path, but His grace is a broad plain.

The evidence is plain—you cannot get away from God's grace! So let's hold these two great truths in a marvelous tension. First, God's plan for us is a narrow path; it is very specific, and God has very particular plans for our lives. But second, we do not live under a "one-false-move" theology. We make many mistakes, and God's grace, which is a broad plain, gives us the room to fail, and then calls us back to that narrow path where we find the fullness of His blessing as we fulfill His will for our lives completely.

Our failures need not thwart the purposes of God for our lives. If we will allow Him, He will, with His mighty hand of promotion, keep lifting us into new places of opportunity. But God will not allow you or me to walk in pride and at the same time experience the fullness of His power, glory and the manifestation of His life in a significant way. His grace is extended to the humble—not to the proud.

Daniel humbled himself before God at a difficult time both in his life and in the life of his nation. He, along with the nation of Israel, had been taken captive into Babylon. In this land, under King Nebuchadnezzar, who knew nothing of Daniel's God, God promotes Daniel along with three of his companions. Daniel comes under the mighty hand of God, and God's mighty hand comes under Daniel.

> Now God had brought Daniel into… favor and goodwill… As for these four young men [Daniel, Shadrach, Meshach and Abed-Nego], God gave them knowledge and skill in all literature and wisdom; and Daniel had understanding in all visions and dreams.… And in all matters of wisdom and understanding about which the king examined them, he found them ten times better than all the magicians and astrologers who were in all his realm.
>
> —Daniel 1:9, 17, 20

These four young men were humbled under the mighty hand of God, and God gave them divine, supernatural abilities that caused them to exceed the skill and ability of Babylon's best wise men ten times over. Babylon was the greatest kingdom on earth in those days, so King Nebuchadnezzar's own magicians and conjurers should have been the world's finest—more highly skilled than the Hebrews. Yet in these verses above, the king is saying instead, "These Hebrew guys *are amazing!*"

Wouldn't that be a wonderful thing for the world to say, recognizing that God in us is greater than what the world's best have to offer? Daniel would not bow the knee to anyone but God. Because he doesn't, God raises him up, and the king takes notice that he is ten times better than any of his own men.

Daniel passed the king's test in these verses. He and his three companions got higher scores than the king's best. But Daniel's wisdom extended far beyond his ability to ace a test—Daniel would soon prove the effectiveness of his wisdom to deal with the day-to-day concerns affecting King Nebuchadnezzar.

One night Nebuchadnezzar had a dream that troubled him. He did not understand what the dream meant, so he called for his wise men to interpret it. Upon hearing it, none of them knew what it meant, and they tried to excuse their lack of wisdom by saying that no one—except the gods—could declare its meaning.

Wrong answer, guys.

In verse 12 we read that Nebuchadnezzar became furious

over their excuse. He ordered that all the wise men of Babylon be executed. The edict included Daniel and his three Hebrew friends. Upon hearing about the king's order, Daniel made an urgent special request:

> So Daniel went in and asked the king to give him time, that he might tell the king the interpretation. Then Daniel went to his house, and made the decision known to Hananiah, Mishael, and Azariah, his companions, that they might seek mercies from the God of heaven concerning this secret, so that Daniel and his companions might not perish with the rest of the wise men of Babylon.
>
> —Daniel 2:16–18

God revealed Nebuchadnezzar's mystery to Daniel in a night vision, and Daniel praised God. Now he could demonstrate the wisdom God had given to him by interpreting the king's dream—and use that opportunity to tell this heathen king about the power of his God. Because he had humbled himself before God, God's mighty hand on his life promoted him before the king, gave him favor with the king, introduced the king to the one true God and spared his life.

Demotion That Leads to Promotion

When you come under the mighty hand of God, the mighty hand of God comes under you. That's the way it works. But sometimes God chooses to take us down before He lifts us up. But if He does, it is because the road to our promotion must first pass through demotion.

In Genesis 37–39 we read how God raised Joseph up out of obscurity. While still a young boy, God gave Joseph a dream filled with great significance. Still young and maybe even a little unwise, in his excitement about the dream Joseph started telling his dream to people. He told his older brothers that his dream was about them bowing down to him, that he would be reigning and they would bow to him one day.

That was when his troubles started. His brothers resented him. They were jealous of him, even hated him for what he told them. They captured him and sold him into slavery in Egypt. There he was imprisoned for years. But during it all, Joseph continued to trust God. Ultimately, although he had to pass through God's season of demotion first, God exalted Joseph to a political rank that would determine the destiny of the nation of Israel.

Sometimes God chooses to take us down before He lifts us up.

While in prison, Joseph, like Daniel, was called by the king to interpret a dream. And because Joseph, like Daniel, used his wisdom to point the king to his powerful God, that heathen king acknowledged the one true God and exalted Joseph to the position of second in command over all of Egypt.

> And Pharaoh said to his servants, "Can we find such a one as this, a man in whom is the Spirit of God?" Then Pharaoh said to Joseph, "Inasmuch as God has shown you all this, there is no one as discerning and wise as you. You shall be over my house, and all my people shall be ruled according to your word; only in regard to the throne will I be greater than you." And Pharaoh said to Joseph, "See, I have set you over all the land of Egypt."
>
> —GENESIS 41:38–41

Because Joseph had humbled himself under the mighty hand of God, he was lifted up to became one of the highest-ranking rulers in Egypt in his day. And before long God fulfilled Joseph's earlier dream as a young boy. During the famine that had been forecast in Pharaoh's dream, Joseph's brothers traveled to Egypt to buy food. As they bowed themselves before him, Joseph revealed himself to them and became God's instrument of mercy to his family and to the nation of Israel.

God made sense to Joseph of his years of demotion by giving him a powerful concept, one Joseph eventually shared with his brothers. As they knelt before him, he told them, "You meant evil against me; but God meant it for good, in order to bring it about as it is this day, to save many people alive" (Gen. 50:20).

Even things happening in your life that appear to be painful for you are somehow in God's plan for you. He is going to turn that around for good in your life.

How to Handle Promotion

When you really begin to live this way, you will find yourself not being able to take credit for your achievements any longer. So if you enjoy taking the credit, you have a choice: be lifted up and maintained by your own human hand and whatever your human hand can do for you, or be lifted up by God, who says, "Not only will I lift you up above and beyond where you could ever lift yourself, but I will also keep you there after I have lifted you up."

God will not take second place. His righteous requirement is that He have *first place* in your life in everything. He will not be second to anything or anyone else, because if people—either believers or unbelievers—look to self first and to Him second, then there is a very good chance that they will miss Him completely because all they will see is self. People can become so enamored with themselves that they will miss Him.

But the Bible admonishes us "not to think of himself more highly than he ought to think" (Rom. 12:3). Anything that God does for you or me is a good thing, a great thing, an awesome thing. But when we start thinking, *I should be doing more... I should have a higher position*, we need to stop and remember that God exalted us to the position we have—it was not of our own doing. Without God we are nothing.

God says that He will lift us up and promote us if we will just say, "Whatever You give me to do, God, I will do it with all my heart." Each of us needs to look at what God has given us to do and say, "That's big!" We need to live in mutual respect of one another and of the grace of God in one another's lives. If that means God chooses to give us a big platform, then we are privileged to be there. But if God chooses to give us a smaller platform, ultimately that's big, too.

God will not take second place. His righteous requirement is that He have first place in your life in everything.

God wants you to get comfortable in your own skin and in your own calling. He also wants you to bring the sum of who you are and put it under His lordship. Then He will be able to promote you and lift you up to whatever position He chooses.

God Has Not Lost Your Address

Each of our lives needs to be the *story of His glory*. They do not need to be about what we did, how we made it, what happened as we did this or that or what we did when we saw this opportunity. Unbelievers talk that way. The people of God talk about what God has done from them.

The apostle Paul is a wonderful example of a man who was thoroughly unenamored with himself and fully giving glory to God. Though one of the greatest missionaries that ever lived—indeed, one of the greatest men of God—at the end of his life he said:

> As for me, God forbid that I should boast about anything except the cross of our Lord Jesus Christ. Because of that cross, my interest in this world died long ago, and the world's interest in me is also long dead.
>
> —Galatians 6:14, NLT

Follow the example of this mighty man of God. In your church, humble yourself before God and before the leadership God has placed you under. When you are ready to be released into a ministry, they will see it. Do not think that God is so limited that He is not able to bring you to the attention of the leaders in your church (remember Sue's story). Do not think

God is so limited that He couldn't just tap somebody on the shoulder and speak to him or her about you.

Do not think God has lost your address—as if you have moved and He never got a change of address card from you. He isn't in heaven saying, "Anybody know what happened to that pastor, Dale Evrist? Anybody know what happened to that student, Donna? Anybody seen that mall clerk, Michael?"

"Nope."

"Oh well, let's not worry about them right now. We have other people to raise up right now."

God is not saying that about you or me or anybody else. God knows how to get us where He wants us to be. He knows how to show leaders the things about us that they need to see.

So do not come under the hand of somebody who is trying to lift you up and exalt you in a world system that is passing away. Instead, come under the mighty hand of God and let *Him* promote you. Let Him lift you up and exalt you.

Your life will be fuller and richer, and so will the lives of the people you touch.

Love of a Thousand Lifetimes

To Abraham You showed Yourself as God and faithful friend;
You promised him a son within the year.
To Sarah, old and barren, You said time and again,
I'll fill you full of laughter all will hear.

You're the love of a thousand lifetimes;
You're the song of a thousand rhymes.
You're the light of a thousand mornings;
You're the star in a thousand skies.

—Lyrics by Dale Evrist and Michael Merritt

Chapter 6

A Hand of Provision

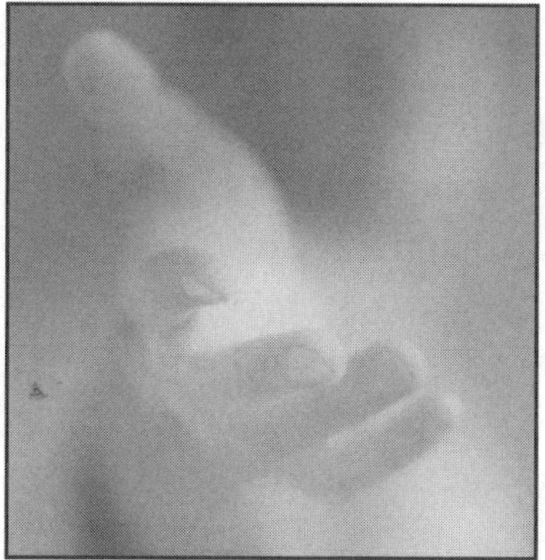

When Cathy* got married, she thought she was living a dream come true. As far as she was concerned, her husband deserved his place on the pedestal on which she placed him. He was her provider, the one who gave her peace of mind, her protector and the one who gave her purpose in life. He was the most fulfilling person in her life, and there was nothing she liked more than being with him. Unfortunately, at that time in her life, Cathy could not say the same thing about God.

According to her, she was in love with herself and her husband—in that order. God was someone she liked, but she could not say she loved Him.

* not her real name

She had made her decision to marry without praying much about it. She believed she knew what she needed in a husband, and the way she looked at it, God wanted her to be happy, so why would He object to her marriage?

Married life turned out to be very satisfying for Cathy. Cathy had been very successful in the entertainment industry before she married, but her husband now took care of making a living for the two of them.

For a while, life seemed perfect for her—but the bliss did not last.

Ten years into her marriage, Cathy's husband left her for another woman. And when her world collapsed, she fell hard. Suddenly, she was faced with the consequences of the decision she had made to take marriage into her own hands.

It was not long before she had been stripped of everything that mattered to her. Gone were her peace, provision, purpose and emotional security. She had no job, and she did not have enough child support or alimony to cover her basic living expenses.

Cathy spent hours lying prostrate before God, crying, "I am ready to look completely to You now. I know You have forgiven my sins. I humble myself before You and ask You to keep Your promises in Your Word and take care of me."

Totally humbled before God, Cathy faced up to her difficulties by submitting herself 100 percent under the mighty hand of God.

And when she did, her life changed radically.

On the day Cathy went to court to finalize her divorce, more than a dozen people were praying that the judge would act favorably on her behalf. The judge not only ruled in her favor on certain financial agreements, but he also gave her two financial advantages for which she had not asked.

With her marriage legally over, Cathy prayed that God would give her His purpose for her life. God led her to start what became a successful business, which she later sold to take a job that provided even more financial security for her. Within a year, she had no debt except for her mortgage. She even managed to save a significant amount of money—something new for her because she and her husband had never saved and were always paying large credit-card debts. After three years, she had paid off her mortgage.

Today Cathy's attitude is that if the tragedy of her marriage was necessary for God to get her where He wanted her to be, then it was worth it. Her testimony now is that God truly lifted her up in her time of trouble as she learned to stay under His mighty hand.

It wasn't always easy, but now she has a clear purpose and vision for what God wants for her. She is healthy emotionally and spiritually, and she is at peace. God has shown her that *He* is her husband, her provider, her peace, her protection and her purpose.

God the Provider Has No Problems, Only Plans

When we talk about God's hand of provision, what are we really saying? Basically, coming under God's hand of provision means we are trusting God to be our provider in everything and to be the one who meets our spiritual, emotional, relational and financial needs.

Realize that God has no problems, only plans.

Cathy had to endure a personal tragedy before her relationship with God became what it needed to be all along—a life lived in complete submission to His will. When she finally put her life in God's hands, He lifted her up, provided for her emotionally, spiritually and financially and gave her—in her own words—"a clear vision" for what He wanted to do in her life.

Doesn't that sound like the God you want to know?

God is always *very clear* about what He is doing. If we will submit to Him and His plans and His purposes for our lives, what happened for Cathy will happen for you. God is not a respecter of persons. That means:

- God knows what He is doing in your life.
- You do not have to be concerned whether He is aware of the events in your life—He is.
- You do not have to be concerned whether He knows what *to do* about your life—He does.
- You do not need to be concerned whether He has the power to accomplish His will—He does.

Realize that God has no problems, only plans. Nothing ever catches God by surprise. God never says, "Whoa! I never saw that one coming." God never wrings His hands and says, "What in the world am I going to do now?"

I want you to understand that God is absolutely sure that He is able to accomplish what He intends to do in your life.

When Cathy submitted her life fully under God's mighty hand, He immediately enacted a plan to provide for her. And He was not worried about whether or not His plan would work. Again, remember, God has no problems, only plans.

He was absolutely sure His plan for her would work. And it did!

God, in effect, was saying to Cathy after her husband left her: "There is no way you can provide completely for yourself—financially or otherwise—so don't even try. Just serve Me. Seek Me first and My kingdom agenda, and then *everything you need* from My hand will be poured into yours." (See Matthew 6:33.)

When Cathy placed herself in God's care, she started to encounter several characteristics of God's hand of provision, and each of them changed her life—ultimately drawing her into a close and intimate relationship with God.

God wants us to experience those same life-giving attributes. He wants us to know that He is our *source;* He *supplies* what we need. He is a God of *increase;* He gives us *abundant*—not *redundant*—life. He replaces our *poverty mentality* with His *abundance mentality.* He makes us a *blessing.* He asks us to *trust* Him, and He uses *whatever means He chooses* to provide for us.

The Baby, the Bath Water and the Blessing

Perhaps by now you're saying, "Oh, great, here is another book that is going to tell me that God wants me to be a millionaire and take the message of prosperity to unbiblical extremes." But I would encourage you to be very, very careful not to throw out the proverbial baby with the bath water and ultimately miss the blessings God has for you.

Yes, it's true that in certain cases people have abused the truth about prosperity. But just because there has been some abuse, do not allow that to lead you away from this truth—God does truly want to bless and prosper you and provide everything you need.

No, God is not going to make everyone a millionaire, though He does that with some people. No, not everyone of us is going to have exactly the same things. But an honest understanding of Scripture reveals this fact: If earthly fathers know how to give good gifts, then how much more will our heavenly Father give good things to him who asks? (See Matthew 7:11.)

God gives us abundant—not redundant—life.

Again, the issue is not whether or not God will make everyone a millionaire—because He won't. The issue is that Jesus said God is far greater than even the biggest-hearted earthly father when it comes to knowing how to give good gifts to those who ask Him.

God always has everything that you and I will ever need. I think He knew that most of us would have a real problem with money.

We would want to rely on it; we would want to work hard to get more of it. We would want to judge ourselves and others by how much of it we have, and we would want to look to it for security instead of being all-dependent on God as our source for everything. That is the very reason why Jesus Himself said in Matthew 6:24 that we cannot serve two masters—God and money.

Money *is* a powerful resource, but the Bible makes it clear that the *love of it* is the root of all kinds of evil (1 Tim. 6:10).

During all the Y2K talk, a television commercial aired showing a guy stepping out of his house on January 1, 2000. Missiles were flying, power was out everywhere and cars were out of control, crashing into one another.

Then the same guy came across an ATM machine that was just shooting money out. Naturally, people were scrambling, trying to grab as much cash as they could carry before the freebie ended. He joined in—knowing the freak chance to get some fast cash would not last long.

Some of us act that way with God. We act as if, for a few minutes during a freak episode of blessing, that God will pour out a big freebie for us, and we had better be ready to hop on it while the getting's good or miss out completely. But God never said He would pop open an ATM machine for us and pour out more dollars than we can haul off.

He actually said something even better.

In Malachi 3:10 God says that He will open the "windows of heaven" (which is a whole lot better than any ATM machine) and pour out a blessing on us that we cannot even imagine.

> "Bring all the tithes into the storehouse, that there may be food in My house, and try Me now in this," says the Lord of hosts, "if I will not open for you the windows of heaven and pour out for you such blessing that there will not be room enough to receive it."

This verse is a challenge for us to trust God. It says, "Test Me and see whether I'll provide for you."

Tithing is one of the indications that you and God have entered into a covenantal relationship. When you receive your paycheck, if anything less than the tithe is given to God (as most of you know, *tithe* means "tenth"), then what you have really done is taken your finances out from under the mighty hand of God.

If you want your finances under God's mighty hand, then bring your tithes into the storehouse (your local church), which is the starting point of trusting God with our finances.

I am not saying that tithing is a license for you to spend money any way you like because it protects you from ever being in debt. That kind of spending is foolish. Your tithe is not a hedge against foolishness.

And do not go charging the limit on your credit card and just say, "God will provide!" That is also foolishness. Tithing is not a hedge against foolishness or disobedience.

Still, God is not one to say to us, "Test Me," and have no idea of how He plans to respond to His own challenge. God is *sure* about what He can and will do.

Tithing is one of the indications that you and God have entered into a covenantal relationship.

It is wonderful to know that you and I can go to bed at night and not lose sleep over how we are going to pay our bills. Instead, we can know that God will provide for us abundantly—with all the things that we need... ever.

One reason we can be sure of this is because God has a great track record of providing for His people when they live in covenantal relationship with Him. Many of you have put God to the test and done exactly what Malachi 3:10 says, and you have watched God bless you abundantly over and over again.

I have had that experience also. God has provided for my needs, and He will always provide for the needs of anyone who is willing to put his or her finances under His hand.

There is no need to worry about whether or not our family bills will be paid or whether or not we will withstand the pressures of our jobs, because we are working the jobs that God has provided for us.

Additionally, the Scripture tells us that when it is God who is providing for His people, He doesn't add sorrow to His provision—He adds "blessing."

> The blessing of the Lord makes one rich, and He adds no sorrow with it.
>
> —Proverbs 10:22

So what does that mean? It means that you and I do not have to worry over the things that God has provided for us. What God provides He also preserves and protects.

That's not a roundabout way of saying you do not have to work. But believing that you have to go out and make things happen for yourself is not the best way. You do not have to go out and make it happen; you need to go out and *watch* it happen. You can be a part of what God is making happen on your behalf.

You will still have to work hard. But if you are living life in partnership with Him and trusting Him for His provision, God will do so much more than you ever imagined. As Romans 8:32 says:

> He who did not spare His own Son, but delivered Him up for us all, how shall He not with Him also freely give us all things?

The fact is, *everything* that we need, God's grace and mercy will supply for us. God's hand of provision is always full. He *never* lacks.

God Supplies What We Need

For some of us, the biggest block we have in our relationship with God is our wallets. If money is the most important thing you have—that thing you love and look at, that thing that you have in the bank and worry about all the time—then you will *never* surrender it to God.

But why are you worried about it? God isn't. He knows that He can provide for you, *with or without your money.*

You may be afraid to tithe because you are on disability. Tithe on your disability.

You may be afraid to tithe because you are on welfare. Tithe on your welfare income.

You may be afraid to tithe because you are on unemployment right now. Tithe on your unemployment income.

You may be afraid to tithe because you have gotten yourself into debt. There is no better way to get out of debt than to tithe on your increase and live within your means. God then will begin to bless you and provide for you the very funds that you need to get yourself out of debt.

Step out in faith and make the sacrifice for God. God is *absolutely* sure that He can provide for you.

God's hand of provision is always full. He never lacks.

I can hear you saying to me now, "Oh no, Dale. I just don't have that kind of money. You don't understand. I'm on a fixed income."

Well, your income is going to stay fixed until you find out it is actually broken, and then you are going to understand how broken your fixed income really is without the tithe!

Tithe if you want to see your fixed income grow. You have to have faith in God that He isn't trying to "steal" from you. God did not send Jesus to steal from you. Jesus came so that we all could have life "more abundantly."

> The thief does not come except to steal, and to kill, and to destroy. I have come that they may have life, and that they may have it more abundantly.
>
> —John 10:10

Jesus says the thief—Satan—is the one who comes to steal. God does not come to you to steal from you. Jesus said He has come to you that you might "have." The only things Jesus came to cause any of us to lose are sin, death, hell and a hopeless, purposeless life.

God Is a God of Increase

Maybe as you are reading this you are thinking, *I thought this was a teaching on provision.* It is, but provision comes to you when you obediently surrender to the will and purposes of God. And part of the way in which you do that, thus opening the door for provision, is by laying your sacrifice on the altar. You may be saying, "Well, Dale, listen. I've sown a lot of good seed financially, and I haven't seen the full harvest. Where is it?"

I would answer you with the Word of God: In due time you will reap.

> And let us not grow weary while doing good, for in due season we shall reap if we do not lose heart.
>
> —Galatians 6:9

Others of you might be saying, "I've been working on this for so long. I sense God's grace. And the Bible is clear that I'm to go on with this. But it just feels like we've been struggling for so long."

Again, the Word of God says that in due time you will reap. Just don't lose heart. Now obviously I am not just talking about tithing here—I am talking about giving. I love the title of Pastor Jack Hayford's book, *The Key to Everything.* He talks about giving as the key to everything, and I could not agree more. In order to see God's provision in everything, we have to be willing to give in everything. This includes our time, talent and our treasure—whether that treasure is monetary or something else that has value to us. God was declaring this truth to Abraham in Genesis 22:16–17 after Abraham had prepared to sacrifice Isaac, the most precious treasure he had, at God's command:

> I have sworn, says the LORD, because you have . . . not withheld . . . your only son—blessing I will bless you, and multiplying I will *multiply* your descendants as the stars of the heaven and as the sand which is on the seashore; and your descendants shall possess the gate of their enemies.
>
> —EMPHASIS ADDED

God told Abraham, "I will . . . *multiply*."

Now, I'm no mathematician, but the statement "I will . . . multiply"—when God says it—sounds like something incredibly exponential to me. God is saying to Abraham, "Exponentially from heaven, I am such a multiplier that in multiplying, I will greatly multiply you." Now, that's a "new math" that I think all of us can live with!

That means He keeps increasing the blessing. After a while it increases to the next mathematical power, then to the next power, then to the next and so on.

That's what happened with Abraham.

According to Galatians 3:7, you and I and anyone who belongs to Christ are the "seed" in Genesis 22:17 that God was talking about.

> Therefore know that only those who are of faith are sons of Abraham.
>
> —GALATIANS 3:7

Think about it: Thousands of years after the conversation God had with Abraham in Genesis 22, God is still multiplying Abraham's seed. He has not stopped increasing Abraham's blessing. And you and I are the recipients of it.

ABUNDANCE VS. REDUNDANCE

I believe God was blessed Himself with the idea of blessing Abraham. I believe that because He loved Abraham and had made a covenant with him—two things that He has done in our lives, too. God wanted to do something for Abraham. He wanted to give to Abraham in a way that was bigger than Abraham's expectation.

Any of us who have children enjoy blessing them at Christmas and at birthdays in whatever way we can. It gives us great joy as parents when we are able to bless our children beyond their expectations. We enjoy it, and they enjoy it. We are blessed because we have been able to bless them.

And of course God is the same way—He is actually the one who has placed in us the desire to bless others.

When He can bless us, it blesses Him. And then He blesses us that we might bless others. In John 10:10, Jesus didn't say, "I came that they may have life, and that they may have it more *redundantly.*"

Again, Jesus did not come to give you redundant life—just the same old same old. He came to give you life that's rich, life that you can get excited about, that you can give your own life to. He came to give you something fabulous.

God has incredible plans and purposes for our lives. He wants to make us signs and wonders. He wants to make our lives a sign that truly makes people wonder.

And of course then our lives become a sign that points beyond ourselves unto Him.

He wants to make our lives a sign that truly makes people wonder.

Your life can be a fabulous adventure, one where you are in partnership with the living God, with Him providing everything you need to carry out the task of living for Him in the world. But you must press in to believe that when Jesus says He came to give us life abundantly, overflowing, that is exactly what He means. And you must be open and ready to receive it—spiritually, emotionally, financially and relationally.

Again I remind you that Romans 8:32 asks the question pretty direct: If God did not withhold His only Son, then won't He freely give us all things through His Son? And the answer to that is, *absolutely.*

Now let me also hasten to say that a view of God's hand of provision giving us abundantly everything that we need, of course, is relative from person to person, place to place, culture to culture, situation to situation. For example, prosperity may be whatever a missionary might have need of in a Third World nation, or whatever would represent abundance or prosperity for someone living in a Third World nation. The Scriptures cannot lie. It is consistent that God, in every situation for everyone who asks, gives us everything that we need—and enough to share and give away.

Abundance Mentality vs. Poverty Mentality

Some of us need to change our view of God. God is not some stingy Father in heaven saying, "Here's just enough. Now, you be happy with that. It's just enough, but that's all you need."

God is not a miser. You can come to the Lord, hold up your bowl and say without fear, "Please, Sir, may I have more?"

And He will say, "More? Absolutely! And not only more for you, but here's even more that you can share with others."

We need to learn to live as people who reject a *poverty mentality* and embrace an *abundance mentality.* A poverty mentality says, "There is never going to be enough." An abundance mentality says, "My God's hand is always full to meet my needs and the needs of others."

My wife, Joan, has taught me a lot about the generous heart of God. There was a lot I needed to learn in that regard! For a long time, God would bless me, but I would feel guilty about it. I would say, "I shouldn't have that car. I just shouldn't have it." What I had wasn't even a big luxury car, though there isn't anything wrong necessarily with having one of those.

When we moved to Nashville from Southern California, God provided a home for us that we could minister in. We use our home a lot for ministry, and God provided a marvelous place for that ministry to be facilitated.

But for the first couple of weeks after we moved in, I struggled, thinking I should not have this home even though it was very clear it was God who had supplied. Although God was blessing me abundantly, I kept yielding to the temptation to think that I did not deserve it. And while, on one hand, it's true that we do not deserve God's blessings, on the other hand we do have a generous God who desires to bless us, and we simply need to say, "Thank You."

My wife has never had a problem believing God wanted to bless her abundantly. Her view of God is really refreshing. She believes God is very generous. Because He loves her, why wouldn't He do nice things for her?

You know what? *She's right.*

Her faith has taught me a lot about the graciousness and generosity of God. He blesses us, but sometimes we tend to live in our extremes.

When God gives you more than you can contain, give it away.

"God," we say, "You're *never* going to do *anything* for me!"

Or we bounce to the other extreme and say, "God, I don't deserve this. I don't know what to do with it."

Well, here's the answer: Just *receive it* with extreme gratitude.

God is a generous God. He isn't a wasteful God, so all of us have to ask Him when enough is enough. That's part of the challenge of receiving God's provision. God is generous, and His provision is abundant.

Let me encourage you who may be bound in a cycle of poverty. Please do not misunderstand what I am saying here. I am not trying to hurt you; I am trying to help you. And I hope that if you live in poverty you will realize that poverty is not God's plan and destiny. Your destiny is not destitution.

Simply release whatever represents a tithe for you; release

whatever represents generosity, and know that as you do, step by step God is going to bless your life.

Blessed to Be a Blessing

God's provision is so abundant, in fact, that He will pour out such a blessing for us that we will not have room to contain it. That means His blessing was meant to overflow the banks of our lives and flow in to bless the lives of others.

He gives us more than we can contain so the blessing will spill out on others. The problem with many of us is that we try to build bigger containers for ourselves rather than giving away the overflow.

But trying to build bigger containers so we can have all the blessing actually blocks the flow that God wants to establish in our lives. When God gives you more than you can contain, give it away.

The Bible says it is more blessed to give than to receive (Acts 20:35). If you will allow God to do so, He will continue to provide for you in greater and greater abundance so that you can then be one of His channels to bless the lives of others. This is the pattern of the kingdom: "Give, and it will be given to you: good measure, pressed down, shaken together, and running over" (Luke 6:38).

Consider yourself to be one of Abraham's sons or daughters. The same promises of the Abrahamic covenant belong to you—and to me. God desires to bless us abundantly so that we can be an abundant blessing.

You Can Trust God

Even though God wants to provide so much for us that we can't contain His blessing, trusting God is the one area that gives many of us the most trouble. Some of us do not know how to trust God, and some of us just do not want to.

In my twenty years as a pastor, I have known people who were susceptible in this way when it came to marriage or friendships or any number of interpersonal relationships. I have known some who, much like Cathy, made big mistakes because they decided God needed their help to accomplish what He had promised about marriage.

God is absolutely sure of what He is doing—all the time and in every situation.

The conversation with God (let's say from a woman's perspective) could go something like this:

"God, I'm in my thirties, OK? That ticking sound You hear is my biological clock." *Tick, tick, tick, tick.* "I'm starting to get those tiny little lines around my eyes."

"Please don't help Me," God says.

"God, I'm starting to get desperate here. Any man breathing and wearing slacks will be fine."

"Please don't help Me," God says.

"God, I'm wondering: Is he even alive? Does he even want to marry me?"

"Please don't help Me," God says. "I know the plans that I have for you, and they're good."

Then in desperation we take matters in our own hands. "Oh, hi! Do you want to marry me? You do? OK, then, let's go."

And God is pleading, "Please don't help Me. Don't settle for something less than what I want to provide for you. I've called you with a different calling. This man is headed in an entirely different direction."

"That's OK, God. It'll all work out somehow. You'll see."

She is right. God does see. He sees the problems that woman is about to get herself into. That's why He told her, *"Please don't help me."*

God is not pacing back and forth in heaven, wringing His hands, saying, "I hope I can supply this. I really *hope* I can supply this. My daughter over here wants a godly husband. There are so few. Where will I find one? I'm not sure I can do it!"

Nor is He saying, "Son, I know I've called you to the

mission field. But I'm...well...I'm having some *trouble* finding the kind of woman who is willing to make that sacrifice with you. All I've got are a few women who would never be willing to pay that kind of price."

Neither of those examples represents an accurate picture of God. God is *absolutely* sure of what He is doing—all the time and in every situation.

Remember, God has no problems, only plans. His plan is that you might *have*, according to His will and under His hand of provision.

People Are Not Your Source—They Are God's Channels

It was my good friend Pastor Wayne Cordeiro whom I first heard use the following expression: "People are not your source; they are God's channels." I loved it when I heard it, and so now I'll borrow it from Wayne because I think it speaks so well to God's hand ultimately being the hand of provision for all of us.

So, when we talk even in terms of us providing for our own needs, or of a man providing for his own family, ultimately we need to understand that it is God who is the ultimate provider. God is using a married man's job as a channel to meet those needs. Yes, the Bible says in 1 Timothy 5:8, "If anyone does not provide for his own, and especially for those of his household, he has denied the faith and is worse than an unbeliever." But we should never forget that it is God who has provided what we need personally and for our families. We simply are taking the initiative to accept what has come to us from God's hand in heaven.

Your source is not man. Man is only a channel.

When you go to work, you are not working for your source. You are working for someone who is a channel.

Your source is the hand of God, and the channel is *any way* and *anyone* God chooses to use to give you what you need. If you think that by your own strength and the sweat of your own brow you are bringing home what your family needs, then you are living life the hard way.

That is not the way we want to live. We want to live in the knowledge that whatever we receive for ourselves, or that we deliver to our families, comes ultimately from the hand of God. In the next chapter we will look at three vital principles we need to know to see God's hand of provision released in our lives.

Love of a Thousand Lifetimes

As Isaac climbed the mountain, the wood upon his back,
His father following the Great I Am,
The son said to the father, "Where's the sacrifice we lack?"
The father said, "Let's trust His mighty hand."

You're the love of a thousand lifetimes;
You're the song of a thousand rhymes.
You're the light of a thousand mornings;
You're the star in a thousand skies.

—Lyrics by Dale Evrist and Michael Merritt

Chapter 7

How God's Provision Is Released in Our Lives

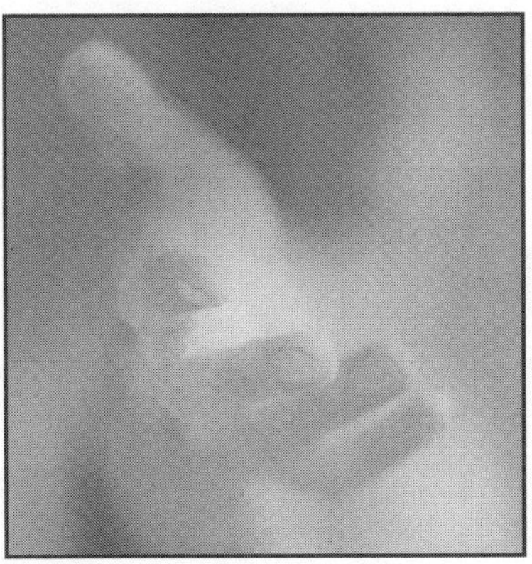

As a Christian, you will face situations in which God seems to be asking more of you than you can give. You may face times, perhaps you already have, when God will ask you to lay down things that He has given you—things that you have believed Him for.

"God, what are You doing?" you will ask, bewildered. "I'm right at the verge of seeing this thing happen, and now You're telling me to lay it down? I don't get it."

I have known a number of Christian music artists as well as other public performers, ministers, professional people and business people who served in their positions for a good long time. But a point in their lives came when God asked them to lay down what they had been doing. He directed that they take a different position, mentoring and helping to release younger people either to do the very things these people had been doing for so many years or to serve in some other way.

That's a challenge for people who for years have strapped on a guitar, stepped out on center stage and picked up a microphone to sing before crowds of people. It's also a challenge for the one who has been doing the pastoring, leading, preaching and teaching. It's also a challenge for those who have been involved in sales, teaching and other professions. Those are positions to which people become accustomed, and it becomes almost an identity badge that says, "This is who I am."

But God knows what He's doing when He changes our course. He sent Elijah to anoint Elisha to take his place, enabling Elisha to have a ministry with twice as many miracles as effective as Elijah. He prevented Paul from following his own itinerary, thus opening up a great revival in an obscure part of the world Paul had not intended to visit. And he directed Paul to mentor a young, sometimes frightened man named Timothy, who became a great church leader.

Three Principles That See God's Provision Released

In the story of Cathy that began in the previous chapter, Cathy learned through her experience to live out the three key principles that release God's hand of provision in all our lives: faith, obedience and persistence.

She came to God in faith when her marriage collapsed, she obeyed what God told her to do and she hung on to God persistently while He provided a new life for her.

In this chapter we will take a close look at these three principles. As we learn to respond to God with faith, obedience and persistence, we will experience His mighty hand of provision blessing our lives abundantly—just as He promised to do in John 10:10.

Faith: Believe It, and You Will See It

> Now faith is the substance of things hoped for, the evidence of things not seen.
>
> —Hebrews 11:1

The Bible is filled with examples of people who exhibited great faith in order to accomplish great things for God. The great faith chapter of Hebrews 11 gives an impressive list of "heroes of the faith." From our great patriarch, Abraham, to nameless saints who were martyred because of their faith, these heroes of the faith were each promoted by God to a position that demanded great faith—even to the point of giving their lives for that faith.

God's hand of provision will never fail the hero of faith! God wants all of us to be great men and women of faith. "Without faith, it is impossible to please Him" (Heb. 11:6).

God knows what He's doing when He changes our course.

Obedience is a big thing to God. The extension of His hand of provision in our direction is dependent upon our obedience to His will and ways. In 1 Samuel 15:22, Samuel asserts:

> Has the Lord as great delight in burnt offerings and sacrifices, as in obeying the voice of the Lord? Behold, to obey is better than sacrifice.

While obeying God in all things is never easy—it is necessary. We step out from under God's hand of provision when we disobey. We get out of the reach of God's mighty hand when we walk the path of disobedience. Saul lost his kingdom through disobedience. Ananias and Sapphira lost their lives because of disobedience.

Choose to obey God in all things. You cannot afford to disobey.

If you will allow God to do so, He will lead you into new days in which your ministry or job profile may change. And He will provide you with the resources you need to mentor a new generation.

When that happens we are tempted to say, "This can't be right." But in God's economy, what looks like loss will lead to gain. We see this exemplified in the life of Abraham when he was faced with the decision to obey God by sacrificing his son Isaac:

> Now it came to pass after these things that God tested Abraham, and said to him, "Abraham!" And he said, "Here I am." Then He said, "Take now your son, your only son Isaac, whom you love, and go to the land of Moriah, and offer him there as a burnt offering on one of the mountains of which I shall tell you."
>
> —GENESIS 22:1–2

Abraham had lived with the heartbreak of Sarah's barrenness for many years before Isaac was born. With only his faith in God to sustain him, Abraham waited for the promise of a son. Was it really possible now that his God was asking Abraham to lose that promise...to give up the son who meant so much to him? And without even an adequate explanation! Abraham could have responded by saying, "Wait a minute, God. Now I know You are usually right, but do You remember how long You made me wait for this boy? And do You remember that You said my descendants would be as numerous as the stars? Surely You don't really mean what You're saying!"

But God did mean it—and Abraham responded in total obedience, even though he was being led down a path that seemed disastrous.

> So Abraham rose early in the morning and saddled his donkey, and took two of his young men with him, and Isaac his son; and he split the wood for the burnt offering, and arose and went to the place of which God had told

> him. Then on the third day Abraham lifted his eyes and saw the place afar off. And Abraham said to his young men, "Stay here with the donkey; the lad and I will go yonder and worship, and we will come back to you."
>
> So Abraham took the wood of the burnt offering and laid it on Isaac his son; and he took the fire in his hand, and a knife, and the two of them went together. But Isaac spoke to Abraham his father and said, "My father!" And he said, "Here I am, my son." Then he said, "Look, the fire and the wood, but where is the lamb for a burnt offering?" And Abraham said, "My son, God will provide for Himself the lamb for a burnt offering." So the two of them went together.
>
> Then they came to the place of which God had told him. And Abraham built an altar there and placed the wood in order; and he bound Isaac his son and laid him on the altar, upon the wood. And Abraham stretched out his hand and took the knife to slay his son.
>
> —Genesis 22:3–10

Still responding in complete obedience, Abraham was ready to plunge that knife deep into the chest of his beloved son in order to obey God. That act of total obedience loosed God's hand of provision for Abraham.

> But the Angel of the Lord called to him from heaven and said, "Abraham! Abraham!" So he said, "Here I am." And He said, "Do not lay your hand on the lad, or do anything to him; for now I know that you fear God, since you have not withheld your son, your only son, from Me."
>
> —Genesis 22:11–12

Now picture this: Abraham and Isaac are climbing up one side of Mount Moriah—walking in faith and obedience to God, ready to make the ultimate sacrifice. At the same time, walking up the other side of the mountain is a ram, probably with the angel of the Lord behind that ram saying, "Get up. Get up there. Get up there in the thicket and stay."

Abraham did not know that was going on as he and Isaac were walking up the mountain. But God knew what was happening. *Jehovah Jireh*—the provider—knew *exactly* what He planned to do.

God knew exactly what He was going to do to spare Isaac's life and provide the sacrificial animal for Abraham. God knew exactly *what* He was going to do and *when* He was going to do it.

> Then Abraham lifted his eyes and looked, and there behind him was a ram caught in a thicket by its horns. So Abraham went and took the ram, and offered it up for a burnt offering instead of his son. And Abraham called the name of the place, The-Lord-Will-Provide; as it is said to this day, "In the Mount of the Lord it shall be provided."
>
> Then the Angel of the LORD called to Abraham a second time out of heaven, and said: "By Myself I have sworn, says the LORD, because you have done this thing and have not withheld your son, your only son—blessing I will bless you, and multiplying I will multiply your descendants as the stars of the heaven and as the sand which is on the seashore; and your descendants shall possess the gate of their enemies. In your seed all the nations of the earth shall be blessed, because you have obeyed My voice."
>
> So Abraham returned to his young men, and they rose and went together to Beersheba; and Abraham dwelt in Beersheba.
>
> —GENESIS 22:13–19

Notice we do not read that the angel of the Lord—running sixty seconds behind schedule—comes along and finds Isaac dead and exclaims, "Oh, gee, I missed my cue! Oh, wow! Oh, this is not good. This is not good *at all.* Uh, has anybody seen God?"

God was not wandering around—in the place He Himself had chosen for Abraham—saying, "Oh, this desolate place, this desolate place! Where in this desolate place, this *Moriah* of all places, am I going to find a ram? Where out here in the middle of nowhere will I ever find a ram?"

God was not saying that—but where *did* He get that ram? How do you break a ram from its herd and send it up a mountain and cause it to be caught in a thicket?

When you are God, that is not really a problem for you. It really isn't.

This shows us that God's provision often is being prepared behind the scenes where we cannot see it or know about it. We will receive it only when we let God be God and walk in faith and obedience.

Gerald Coates, another friend of mine, says, "God is doing more behind our backs than in front of our faces." I really believe that to be true. How many times is God at work, out of our view, doing things of which we are not even aware? Another friend, Ron Mehl, in his book *God Works the Night Shift*, talks about all the things God is doing even when we are asleep.

All Abraham knew was that he was obeying the Lord, doing what God had called him to do. Sometimes we lay down our very best and think, *I don't know how God's going to provide.* But at the right moment we lift our eyes and see that there is a provision. It wasn't there all along, but it was there when we needed it. In the words of the old African American spiritual, "God is never in a hurry, but He's always right on time."

When God seems to be changing the direction of your life, when He seems to be removing you from your calling, just trust Him and obey Him wholeheartedly. You will loose God's mighty hand of provision for your life if you do. He will "open the windows of heaven" and pour out a blessing so much greater than anything you could have imagined or dreamed for yourself.

Obedience: Learning to Pass the Test

When you let go of those things that you love the most, you are committing an ultimate act of worship to the Lord through your obedience. You are letting go of what you prize the most, trusting that the mighty hand of God will give you what you need. This is facing what looks to be a loss, but finding that it leads to gain by making the sacrifice.

If God had said to Abraham, "Lay down Isaac," and Abraham had answered, "No, no. You promised this to me. This is my son. You can't ask this of me. I don't care what You say; this is something I will not obey," then he no longer would have been a candidate for what God ultimately intended to do with his life.

If we do not do what God has given us to do today, then why should He give us the next step of the assignment tomorrow? We will not handle tomorrow properly if we do not handle today properly. We must pass the test of today to move to the graduation of tomorrow.

What if you were a freshman in college, and you said, "Man, I don't want to be a freshman. I want to be a senior. I *should* be a senior. I *deserve* to be a senior." So, you ditch class every day as a freshman, believing that you are smarter and more important than your classmates and deserve to be a senior.

God is doing more behind our backs than in front of our faces.

Guess what? You will not become a senior. You will not even become a *sophomore.* You will always be a freshman until you have done what is required of freshmen to go to the next level.

Could I encourage you to take some time right now and go back to read the first chapter of the Book of James. There it talks about not only passing tests—but approaching them with great joy knowing that God's hand will provide the grace that we need for strength and wisdom to go through whatever God is taking us through.

Do you remember when Elijah became afraid of Queen Jezebel and her threats and fled nearly five hundred miles to hide in a cave (1 Kings 19)? Here are God's first words to Elijah in that cave: "What are you doing here, Elijah?" (v. 13). God had not intended for Elijah to leave the place where He had placed him. Even when Elijah tried to justify his trip by telling God how evil the children of Israel had become, God responded by saying, "Go, return on your way… " (v. 15).

Elijah had to return to the very place where he stepped out of God's plan for his life. Before God would move him from there, he had to pass the test God gave him there. The reason so many people go through the same test over and over and over again is because they have never been *obedient* to God and passed their test. As you are reading this book, you may be right now in the middle of the same test that you have been in time and time again.

Do you want to graduate?

Then pass the test.

The great news is that God wants you to pass the test, and He will support you. He wants it for you so that by His mighty hand He can more fully provide for you. But you must walk in faith, obedience and persistence with Him.

Laying Down Our Isaacs

Abraham is a role model for us in having the kind of trust in God that turns what at first appears to be great loss into great gain. He accepted his assignment from God in faith, was obedient to God's will for his life and was persistent enough to keep on doing God's will, even to the point of sacrificing Isaac.

But let's not kid ourselves.

Abraham did not fully understand what God was doing, and you and I don't either. He wasn't really that much different from us when it came to trusting God. If his faith had been perfected, then God would not have had to test him.

Isaac was the son he and his wife, Sarah, had in their old age—the son God had promised to them years before Isaac's birth. So it would be *unthinkable* that Abraham *wanted* to sacrifice Isaac after God commanded him to.

You and I may face all kinds of tests that are meant to

determine whether or not we ultimately will trust God as our provider, to determine whether or not we are looking to the mighty hand of God.

We must be willing to lay down our Isaacs and trust God to provide everything that we need. Looking at Abraham we see that he simply did what God called him to do.

Letting God Be God: The Place of Faith and Obedience

Abraham believed in God so much that he expected somehow that God would raise Isaac from the dead. He says, "The lad and I will go yonder and worship, *and we will come back to you*" (Gen. 22:5, emphasis added). Abraham had already decided that when it came to Isaac, he was going to trust God in that.

It is interesting that the writer of Hebrews tells us something about this story of Abraham and Isaac that isn't revealed anywhere in Genesis 22:

> By faith Abraham, when he was tested, offered up Isaac, and he who had received the promises offered up his only begotten son, of whom it was said, "In Isaac your seed shall be called," *concluding that God was able to raise him up, even from the dead*, from which he also received him in a figurative sense.
>
> —Hebrews 11:17–19, emphasis added

From the Book of Hebrews we find that Abraham had so much faith in God he believed that—despite the fact the Lord had said to him, "Slay your son, your only son"—God was able to raise Isaac from the dead.

Abraham actually was saying, "Somehow, some way, I don't understand it all, but I know that You promised me Isaac. And I know that You've given me Isaac. And I know that even if Isaac is slain, somehow he'll come back from the dead. I believe in You that much, God."

> And Abraham said, "My son, God will provide for Himself the lamb for a burnt offering."
>
> —GENESIS 22:8

Abraham knew that God would provide, so he obeyed God. He did not know how until the moment he actually raised his knife, but he was sure about God.

What faith that was for a man who did not even have the Scriptures or know anything about Jesus Christ. Abraham did not have the type of revelation that you and I have today as twenty-first-century believers!

Yet with the revelation that Abraham did have, he was willing to lay it all on the line. And when he did—even though he was old and did not seem like a man who had many days left—God told him, "Your best days are ahead of you. In fact, they'll outlive you. What I am going to do in your life will significantly outlive you."

Perhaps you cannot figure out why your life keeps blowing up on you. Over and over again, life thwarts you, frustrates you and keeps you unhappy.

In one way or another, the reason this happens is because we are not doing what God has called us to do. I am not saying that to discourage you, but I am saying that to challenge you to seek God's face as to the better thing He is calling you to. He is patiently trying, again and again, to show you what you *should not* be doing so that you will start seeking what you *should* be doing. This will always lead to blessing in your life.

Maybe you are avoiding what God has called you to do because it isn't in keeping with someone of your "stature." So God continues to deal with you. He tries to teach you that if you would do the work He has given you to do, then you would discover His task for you is good—in fact, the best thing for your life today.

If your present assignment seems insignificant—only a step on the way instead of the destination you'd like—do not give in to the temptation to refuse it.

Wrapped up in God's provision for us are His purposes for us. These purposes will extend far beyond our lifetimes if we obey Him. Today Abraham and Isaac are in heaven. But the promise that in Abraham's seed all the nations of the earth would be blessed is being fulfilled right now through people like you and me. (See Galatians 3:7–9.) That's the power of God's mighty hand of provision.

Persistence: Just Keep Going

Do you remember the persistence of Jacob, who said, "I will not let You go unless You bless me!" (Gen. 32:26)? Jacob came to understand the power of persistence. He believed that receiving God's blessing would only happen if he persisted.

It is often true that persistence comes before provision. Caleb persisted for his mountain. (See Joshua 14:6–13.) The gentile woman with a sick child persisted for her child's healing. When Jesus delayed His hand of healing, she persisted by saying, "Even the little dogs eat the crumbs which fall from their masters' table" (Matt. 15:27). Her persistence got the attention of Jesus.

> Then Jesus answered and said to her, "O woman, great is your faith! Let it be to you as you desire." And her daughter was healed from that very hour.
>
> —Matthew 15:28

God's hand of provision is also released in our lives through persistence. When we look at our lives, or at circumstances in our lives for which we never planned and over which we have no control, it can seem to us as if all is lost. It seems that we will never make it. What needs to happen is not happening for us. What needs to work out is not working out for us.

Maybe you have a word from the Lord. Maybe God has spoken a promise to you. But still it seems to you that all is lost. Hang on to that word from God. Just keep going in the direction of obedience. It will come. It might not come according to the timing you want for it, *but it will not come too late.*

Abraham and Sarah's word from the Lord—their promise from God—applied to a one-hundred-year-old man and a ninety-year-old woman whose bodies were, as the Scriptures say, as good as dead.

After twenty years of pastoring, I have known many people, including myself, who have felt that way. We know what it is to get up in the morning and mutter, "I feel as good as dead." It can seem to us as if all is lost.

Years earlier God had promised Abraham and Sarah that they were going to have a son. And Abraham, like you and me, tried to help God along in His promise. Sarah was an accomplice in the attempt, too. She told Abraham, "Just go in to my maid Hagar. Have a baby with her, and it will be my own." (See Genesis 16:2.) That was an extremely foolish thing to do. Not only was it really sinful, but it was really foolish.

Abraham should have said to Sarah, "I know you really want a baby. But you're not in your right mind now. You're not going to be happy with this. This is not what God has promised us anyway."

It is often true that persistence comes before provision.

Ishmael was born out of Abraham and Sarah's attempt to help God along. We have all produced our "Ishmaels," haven't we?

If you have given birth to your own "son of the flesh" by trying to help God out, then listen up: God does not need your help—or mine. God knows how to do what He is planning to do at the right time. He does not need you to help Him accomplish the prophetic words He has spoken over your life, even if it was so long ago and nothing has happened yet.

God's timing is perfect.

But He needs you to persist...to lift up your eyes and

look... because you are on God's timetable. Chances are, there are things God wants to show you. There are things God wants to teach you. There are areas in which He wants to mature you. God is not asking you to persist in order to punish you; He is asking you to persist so that you will grow in faith and in knowledge of Him.

Instead of keeping busy at being downcast, start looking up. God wants us to know that He has a timetable for the things He wants to do in our lives.

Waiting for the Fullness of Time

Galatians 4:4 tells us that "when the fullness of the time had come, God sent forth His son, born of a woman, born under the law." That means when the time was right, God revealed His Son.

In Andrew Lloyd Webber's musical *Jesus Christ Superstar*, the character Judas audaciously questions Jesus, "Why now? Why would You come now?" He was questioning God's timing when, in retrospect, we can see that God's timing for bringing forth His Son was absolutely perfect.

We need to look in our own lives for the fullness of time. Why? Because God knows how to send His provision when the time is right.

Remember what Jesus said in John 10:10? "I have come that [you] may have life, and that [you] may have it more abundantly."

"I have come," He was saying. He had come in the *fullness* of time. The timing was God's. As Paul said in Galatians 6:9, timing is all-important if we hope to reap God's blessings.

You may have been sowing a long time. You may be wondering if God is ever going to provide that for which you have been believing Him.

Be *filled* with hope—God is fully able to provide for you. Let your heart be filled with hope. In due time you shall reap if you do not lose heart. Jesus made this promise to us in Matthew 7:8:

> For everyone who asks receives, and he who seeks finds, and to him who knocks it will be opened.

In the Greek this means, "Everyone who asks—*and keeps on asking*—receives. He who seeks—*and keeps on seeking*—finds. To him who knocks—*and keeps on knocking*—the door will be opened."

Get under the mighty hand of God. Submit each part of your life to Him. Totally. First, foremost and always, surrender yourself to Him.

Come under His mighty hand of provision and receive all that He has already or will supply for you through the blood of His Son, Jesus Christ. Lack for nothing because He lacks for nothing. No matter what your need...no matter where you are...His hand can reach you.

UNDER YOUR SHADOW

Under Your shadow,
Safe in Your care,
My sacred dwelling,
You'll find me there.
Nothing can harm me,
Nothing to fear.
Under Your shadow
Knowing You're here.

—LYRICS BY DALE EVRIST

Chapter 8

A Hand of Protection

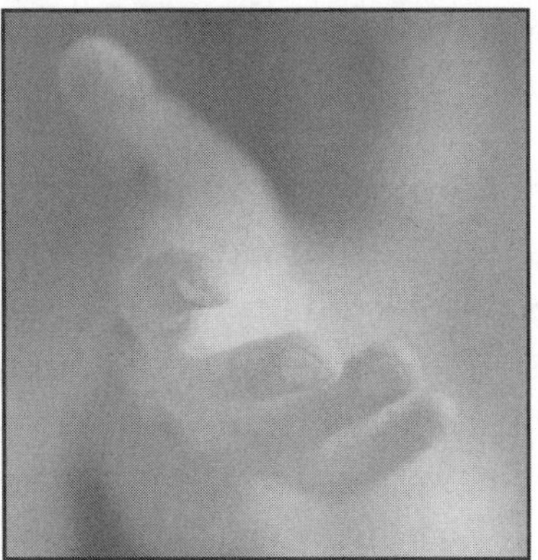

Kyle had been praying for his grandfather for a long time. The tough old man was an ex-Marine who had spent a lot of years working for the railroad, and the hard work and hard living had taken their toll. Kyle's grandfather suffered from emphysema, congestive heart failure, diabetes and other physical ailments.

Kyle knew his grandfather did not have much longer to live. He decided that he needed to make the eight-hour drive from Nashville to Fort Smith, Arkansas, to see the old man. Kyle especially wanted to make the trip to tell his grandfather about Jesus.

On the way to Fort Smith a light rain started to fall that gradually developed into a fierce thunderstorm. Kyle slowed to about fifty miles per hour on the interstate. However, his sport-utility vehicle suddenly began to hydroplane. Within moments he had lost all control of the vehicle as it went into a spin.

The thought raced through Kyle's mind that because his car was very top-heavy, it would surely flip over. As he prayed and clutched the steering wheel, he spun across two lanes of interstate roadway and through the grass median before finally stopping. When Kyle looked around, he realized his vehicle was positioned sideways in the oncoming lanes on the opposite side of the interstate.

God, thank You for keeping my car from flipping! Kyle prayed, relieved.

Kyle felt as if God literally had placed His hand on top of the car to stabilize it during the frightening slide. He also knew that God had protected him from being broadsided as he had spun helplessly into the lanes of oncoming traffic.

His car was not damaged, so as other drivers went around him, Kyle backed up, returned to the other side of the interstate and continued on his way to see his grandfather. His visit turned out to be an appointment that God had not wanted him to miss.

When the servants of God walk in faith and obedience, they are indestructible until God's plan for them is complete.

By the end of Kyle's weekend with his grandfather, he had the privilege of seeing his desire fulfilled. His tough—but now softhearted—old grandfather gave his life to Jesus.

INDESTRUCTIBLE IN GOD'S HAND

That day on the interstate easily could have been Kyle's last. All of us probably have read in the newspaper or seen on the evening news a report about someone who for one reason or another lost control of his car while driving on the interstate, crossed the median to the other side and was struck and killed by oncoming traffic.

Kyle's experience might have turned out to be just another one of those "Details at 11" news reports about a tragic, probably unavoidable accident. But it wasn't. And the reason it wasn't is simple: God protected Kyle.

God was fulfilling for Kyle a critical truth from His Word about those who live under His mighty hand: When the servants of God walk in faith and obedience, they are indestructible until God's plan for them is complete.

That means when you walk in faith and obedience—with your life fully surrendered to Him—then you are indestructible until God's plan for you is finished.

I doubt that Kyle was thinking of Psalm 91 while he was spinning out of control on that rain-slicked highway. But God was thinking about it. Possibly nowhere else in the Bible do we find a more complete description of how God will spare and protect those who entrust their lives to Him than in Psalm 91.

Among a number of things, this psalm makes one fact clear: God *knows* how to take care of His people.

> He who dwells in the secret place of the Most High shall abide under the shadow of the Almighty. I will say of the LORD, "He is my refuge and my fortress; My God, in Him I will trust." Surely He shall deliver you.... You shall not be afraid of the terror by night, nor of the arrow that flies by day, nor of the pestilence that walks in darkness, nor of the destruction that lays waste at noonday. A thousand may fall at your side, and ten thousand at your right hand; but it shall not come near you... Because you have made the Lord, who is my refuge, even the Most High, your dwelling place.
>
> —PSALM 91:1–9

Contained in these verses is a direct statement about God's mighty hand of protection and how it covers and preserves the security of His people. The Septuagint—the ancient Greek version of the Old Testament—credits King David as being the writer of this psalm. It refers to events very similar to the kind David lived through. In language and style it is similar to the things David wrote about and how he wrote about them.

But this psalm is actually anonymous—no writer gets the credit for it. In some ways I think that makes it even stronger. As an anonymous declaration of God's power to protect, it somehow becomes even more applicable to everyone. Because no one knows who wrote it, it can't be applied to only one person's experience. Therefore, it seems easier to think, *You know what? I feel like I could have written this. This really applies to me. This is the kind of thing I feel about my own experience. When I read this, it doesn't just apply to someone in the past, but I really see it applying to me today.*

With God, it's not over until God says it's over.

Psalm 91 was written by a person who had lived through some pretty horrendous times—heavy stuff like disease, pestilence, war, possibly intense daytime and nighttime combat, surprise attacks, traps laid by people with evil intent and massive destructive forces that took other people's lives.

Whoever wrote Psalm 91 had not been through a cakewalk—had not been insulated or spared from some of the roughest stuff life can throw at us. In realizing that, let's not overlook the obvious: Whoever wrote Psalm 91 had *survived* those dangerous times.

This person was writing from *experience.* This person had gone through the heavy stuff. Death had hung around this person's door, waiting for a chance to get in—on many more than one occasion. But it had come up empty-handed every time.

If there's one point the writer of Psalm 91 is trying to make crystal clear, it is this: With God, it's not over until God says it's over.

Putting First Things First

The psalmist declares his confidence in the protection that

comes from abiding in the secret place of God. In verse 2, he says, in effect, "You want evidence for the case? Let me be the first to step up to the witness stand and say, 'He is my refuge and my fortress, my God, in Him I will trust.'"

The writer would not have said this if he had not had the evidence for his case. He would not be a credible, reliable or believable witness if he did not have evidence. But he does. So he testifies in verse 1, "He who dwells in the secret place of the Most High will remain and abide under the shadow of power." The psalmist is sounding a trumpet, saying, "In Him I will trust. I am not going to trust in myself; I am not going to trust man; I am not going to trust human resources. I am going to trust in Him and come under the protective, delivering hand of almighty God. He is the place I run to and find safety—He's my 'refuge,' my heavily guarded walls, my 'fortress.'"

It is pretty easy for us to determine whether or not we are trusting in God when we are under attack. The trouble might be coming from people who do not know God, or it might be coming from fellow Christians.

At times like this, some people function on what I call "soular energy," or soul power. As soon as anything happens in their lives, *boom!* They're online e-mailing someone or calling someone on the phone. They start talking to anybody and everybody except God. God should be the first person we go to when we are in the midst of trouble, if we really are abiding in the secret place of the Most High, under the shadow and wings of the Almighty.

If that's our dwelling, then our declaration is, "Lord, You're my refuge. You are my fortress. You are my God, and I trust You. If You're using this to teach me something, then I trust You that I am going to learn the lessons. And Lord, if this is simply an assault by the devil, then I trust that You, God, are going to protect me. And I look to You, God; I lean into You."

That does not mean that God will not use people to help us. But if you or I run to people at the first sign of trouble in our lives, then we are not dwelling in the secret place of the Most High. We are not under the shadow of the Almighty, and we are not under His wings. We are living on our own, out in the open.

If we take a shot from the devil or from our own hard circumstances, we begin to lean on our understanding and acknowledge *ourselves* and people around us. "I've got to get to my counselor!" we say. "I've got to get to my therapist. I've got to get to my friends."

God should be the first person we go to when we are in the midst of trouble.

Of course, there is nothing wrong with having people in our lives who help us. We all need that, and that is certainly a needed resource for God's delivering work in our lives. But what I want you to ask yourself is this: Do you run to Him *first* when something starts to happen? Are you abiding so much under His mighty hand that the *first* person you run to is God? If you go to God first, then He will show you if you are to go to anyone else and if so, whom. But go to God first. By looking first, foremost and always to the mighty hand of God to protect us, to guard us and to guide us, we find our deliverance.

LIVING IN A DANGEROUS WORLD

Some of us know what it's like to live with disease. Maybe it has touched our own lives, or maybe we have lived with it by watching it affect someone else's life. Some of us have lived through combat or war, or have known people who have. Some of us know what it's like to know that our lives are in danger.

But probably for most of us, the idea of going through a day or night knowing at any moment our life could be taken is a foreign feeling. That's why Psalm 91 is also written for people who do not necessarily live in imminent danger but who live in a dangerous world both physically and spiritually. It's a passage for people who know what it's like to face obstacles in life and feel defenseless and powerless against them.

The experiences that the writer of Psalm 91 lived through are not everyday experiences for most of us. That could be one reason why God allowed that writer to live through such extremes—so that we would see that He is more than able to deliver His people out of the worst things the world has to offer. And we all know, regardless of our life experiences, that the world is not exactly the safest place to live.

The psalmist is saying, "People of God, there is a place where you can live and be secure—no matter what life or the devil or other people bombard you with. It's a spiritual place, but it's every bit as protective as a mountain stronghold. It's called the *shadow of the Almighty.*" It's under the shadow of *Shaddai*, which in the Hebrew means "fortress" or protection. *Shaddai* is the all-sufficient, the all-powerful, the never-had-a-problem-only-have-a-plan God. This is the God who protects us when we come under Him.

And because we are safe and never more secure than when we are under the mighty hand of God's protection, the enemy will resist our living there. Therefore it's wise for us not to forget: We will not be able to live under the mighty hand of God without a challenge.

Was That God's Hand on the Wheel?

I once asked our congregation for a show of hands: "How many of you," I asked, "can say that God preserved you either from death or serious injury? You know it was God's hand that protected you. If He had not protected you, either you would have died or you would have been seriously injured. Let me see your hand."

I was amazed! Hands went up all over the room that morning.

I told them, "It can't be coincidence! Recognizing how many of you have been protected by the hand of God *cannot* be coincidence."

Nearly all of us have seen God's hand of protection.

God spared me once, much as He did Kyle, while I was driving on a freeway in Los Angeles. It had just rained, and the roads were very slick. The woman driving in front of me slammed on her brakes unexpectedly, and I hit my brakes hard to avoid slamming into her.

My car hydroplaned, then spun 180 degrees out of control at fifty-five miles per hour. The only thing I knew to say in that moment was, "Protect me, Jesus!" The next thing I knew the car had flown off the freeway and landed fifteen feet down in a cement drainage ditch that was just big enough for my car.

But I walked away from that accident.

Later I found out that just a short time before the wreck happened, God awakened my sister and told her with an urgency, "Begin to pray right now for Dale and for his protection." I believe that my sister's prayer was part of God's promise that His mighty hand of protection overshadows me and protects my life from ultimate harm.

If God had not protected me that day, what might have happened? I don't know. But add up a busy Los Angeles freeway, a slick, rainy highway, a speed of more than fifty miles per hour and a fifteen-foot drop onto concrete, and you get the picture: The result could have been disastrous—for me as well as for other drivers on the freeway.

Did Satan try to get rid of me that day? Well, whether he did or not, the simple fact is that God protected me. Again, I can tell you that when the servants of the Lord walk in faith and obedience, they are indestructible until God's plan for them is complete.

Off-Road Driving: Unbelief and Disobedience

Notice that I keep saying, "When the servant of the Lord walks in *faith and obedience.*" One of the things you will discover is that the "twin sins" keeping us out of the fullness of God's promise and God's protection are always unbelief and disobedience.

You must be submitted beneath the mighty hand of God. Just

as you are never safer than when you are submitted, so you are never more in trouble than when you are not submitted.

If you do not trust God, if your faith is in yourself and not in God, then you can go only as far as your own ability, strength or power to control your circumstances can take you. There are plenty of believers who cut their lives short because they do not walk in obedience. Others take big risks with their well-being because they tempt God.

You *could* (but I would not advise it) stand on a train track and just say, "I'm going to trust God here. When the train comes, I'm just going to trust God that nothing will happen to me." You aren't *trusting* Him; you are *tempting* Him. And when that train comes—and goes—you are going to be in heaven, and God is going to be asking you, "What were you *thinking?*" If you walk in foolishness, you walk uncovered and out from under the shadow of the Almighty.

Therefore, just as it is possible for us to walk in obedience to God and have His blessings and favor working in our lives, it is also possible to walk in disobedience and have all kinds of bad stuff happen to us. For example, consider what verse 3 of Psalm 91 says, "Surely He shall deliver you from the snare of the fowler."

The psalmist was referring to a type of professional hunter—the "fowler." The fowler trapped birds, and his snares were traps set and individually baited for the particular kinds of birds he hunted.

Do you know that as a believer there are traps out there baited just for you? Satan—the hunter—has designed them with you in mind. They are baited with the things that draw you in, cleverly set up to pull you in by way of your individual personality traits, your spiritual or fleshly weaknesses, your emotional or relational flaws—maybe even through your personal interests.

Do you know what kind of bait attracts you? Do you ever feel that you are baited? Maybe you were baited this week, maybe even today—lured or subtly enticed to go after something that you know isn't spiritually, emotionally or physically healthy for you.

> *Just as you are never safer than when you are submitted, so you are never more in trouble than when you are not submitted.*

Don't be surprised by this. The enemy is not stupid. After all, Jesus called Satan "the *prince* of this world." That's a title given to a ruler, not a clueless buffoon.

The enemy would like nothing better than to ensnare our lives, and he is not going to waste time baiting us with things that do not attract us. He is cunning enough not to offer us something we would find repugnant.

Delivered From Hidden Traps

The good news is in verse 3: "Surely [God] shall deliver you from the snare of the fowler." If we walk in obedience to Him, He promises to deliver us from those hidden traps that have been set out there for us. But if we walk in disobedience to God, the likelihood of our walking right into one of those traps shoots up significantly.

I have seen people of fierce faith who are not afraid of anybody or anything. Well, that's a good thing, but there is a negative side to that, too. There's bait in that attitude, bait to draw people like that into some combative conflict that has nothing to do with what God wants to do in their lives. They wind up fighting a fight that isn't their fight, a fight that isn't worth fighting.

For some people the bait is meddling. A *meddler* is someone who gets involved in things that aren't his or her business. Maybe you meddle. You are quick to take up another person's offense. You harbor that and carry it even though it is an issue between two other people and has nothing to do with you whatsoever.

You need to stay out of it, but you don't. You are being disobedient to God. And because you are being disobedient, you are not abiding in the secret place of the Most High. You are not under the shadow of the Almighty and under His wings.

If you were, when that bait was offered, God would say, "Don't take that. Don't do that. Just be at peace and stay with Me."

And you would answer, "Yes, Lord. Yes, Lord." God is saying in verse 3, "I will deliver you from those hidden traps."

Disobedience leads us out from under His mighty hand where we're uncovered. Then, whatever seems or feels right to us, we do. We get into things that have nothing to do with us; we take up offenses, get bitter and angry and then wonder why our world is always going the way it is.

We wonder why our emotions are always in turmoil. There is always somebody we cannot look in the eye. There is always somebody with whom we have a problem. It is because we have taken the bait.

On the other hand, maybe your personality is very nonconfrontive. The idea of taking somebody on face to face isn't bait for you. So instead of meddling, gossip might be great-tasting bait for you.

It could be that you are very bold, maybe even brazen, when you are talking about a person who isn't around to hear it. But in your heart you know that if that person walked in the door while you were talking about him or her, you would come unglued inwardly. You would probably feel that you were "caught in the act"; maybe you would only be able to manage a feeble greeting like, "Oh, golly… hi… oh… *hi!*"

Gossip may be bait for you. In fact, to a certain degree it is bait for all of us. And we all need to ask ourselves, "What represents bait for me?"

God knows what tempts us. He knows what kind of traps are laid for us. If we will walk with Him, He will deliver us from them.

The psalmist is saying that for every trap that is set for you, God is telling you that He knows how to rescue you from it—and He will, *if* you are under His hand. For every devastating thing that comes against you to steal everything you have as a child of God, God is saying to you, "If you will remain in Me, you *will* be under the shadow of the Almighty."

The great thing about all of this is that we have a God of love who loves us enough to deliver us from the snare of the fowler.

HELP! I'M UNDER ATTACK!

Sometimes when we sense the strategies of the devil being released against us we say things like, "I'm under attack." But what we often imply by saying this is that we are taking the blows and there is nothing we can do about what is happening to us. We are saying, "That's just the way it is—*and the way it has to be.*"

According to the psalmist, that is not true.

The writer of Psalm 91 says God will deliver us from the *plans* of the wicked and evil one as well as from the *plans* of wicked and evil men. But because that deliverance comes from dwelling in the secret place of the Most High, it requires us to seek God's face daily, to live in a vital daily relationship with Him—something not all of us do.

Why *don't* we seek God daily?

Simply because we do not think we have to. Not that any of us would ever verbalize such a notion, but deep within our hearts there is a part of us that thinks that unless we are in the midst of crisis, then we are able to handle a good many of our challenges on our own.

We have a God of love who loves us enough to deliver us from the snare of the fowler.

In doing that, we are letting ourselves be lulled to sleep by a subtle sense of unbelief and disobedience. If you do not believe you need to seek God every day, then you will not apply any faith to do so. If you think you can take care of yourself through thick and thin, then you will not believe there's really any reason to put out the effort to obey God, and you won't.

It's the same way with prayer. We don't pray every day because we do not think we have to. We think we can skip days, skip weeks, skip months without communing with the Lord. Again, these are not things we would verbalize and state as convictions, but our lack of prayer indicates a belief that prayer is not absolutely necessary for remaining under the shadow of the Almighty.

We think because there are enough props in our lives, enough crutches, enough things on which to lean that we can somehow make it alone. Then when we reach the end of ourselves we are faced with the inescapable conclusion that we cannot make it on our own. That's what happened with Cathy in chapter six before she learned that only God could be her provision.

A relationship with God is meant to be something intimate, involved and ongoing—a daily thing. That's where our motivation to place our lives under the mighty hand of God comes from. But without faith in and obedience to God, it just will not happen.

For all of us who are Christians, our passion should be—even if we aren't practicing it perfectly—to obey God and dwell under His mighty hand and under His gift of protection.

The Safest Place in the World

If you want to know safety and peace, undisturbed composure, a place where you are not troubled, where you are not worried, it is in the secret place of the all-sufficient, all-powerful God. See God Himself as your refuge:

> He shall cover you with His feathers, and under His wings you shall take refuge.
>
> —Psalm 91:4

In this verse, the psalmist gives us a picture of a mother bird who, when danger or a storm arises, allows her babies to run under her open wings where she then draws them into a warm and secure place.

Jesus revealed this aspect of God's love and protection when He wept over Jerusalem. The Jews there never understood that God's heart longed for them to come under His refuge and live securely and safely protected by His mighty hand.

> O Jerusalem, Jerusalem, the one who kills the prophets and stones those who are sent to her! How often I wanted to gather your children together, as a hen gathers her chicks under her wings, but you were not willing! See! Your house is left to you desolate.
>
> —MATTHEW 23:37

Rejecting God's offer seems crazy if we really stop and think about His invitation. Jesus was saying to Jerusalem, "Come. Come dwell under My shadow. Come dwell under My wing. It's warm here, and it's safe here. Nothing can hurt you here, and nothing can harm you. Nothing can take away your security. Nothing can take away your peace." Interestingly, they refused His desire for them, and the city later was destroyed by Rome.

God is still inviting us to come under His wings and be protected. Yet, oftentimes we still say, "No, God. I've got this one. Let me take it from here. I know what I'm doing."

And the Lord says, "No, you really don't."

But we insist, "I can protect myself, God. I can protect myself."

As we talked about in chapter six earlier, there was much talk about Y2K and the widespread chaos some people predicted would occur because of the millennium bug computer-programming flaw. The number of firearms being purchased in our country was on the rise. But the secret place of the Most High never has been and never will be "your handgun." You are fooling yourself if you are saying, "The secret place of the Most High is my Glock 9mm pistol underneath my bed. It's in my own personal secret place, so now I feel safe."

Literally and figuratively speaking, somebody always has a bigger gun than you have. Somebody is always bigger, better, stronger and more armed than you are. Always.

Men—especially those of us who are husbands and fathers—have an instinctive desire to protect our families. That is not wrong. That is something God has placed in all of us. But because we do feel this way, sometimes rather than depending on God, we tend to say things like, "You better not mess with my wife. You better not mess with my kids, because I'm going to protect them at any cost."

But we rarely let on that all of our talk of protection of our families on our own is, at some point, irrelevant. For example (if you are a guy, you will understand this!), you may actually take another guy on and get into a fight. That may be your style. But no matter how angry you are, no matter how protective of your family you are, if the other guy tips the scale at 325 pounds, you are going down. You can say all you want, you can make all the threats you want, but you are *done*—you are history, toast, and you are going down on this one.

God is still inviting us to come under His wings and be protected.

If some guy cuts you off in traffic and starts cursing you, it is not going to matter how much you have studied self-defense if he's a mountain of a man. You can make all the fancy karate kicks and sounds that you want—that guy is going to squash you.

If you are not strong enough and well-armed enough to protect even yourself, then how can you expect to protect your family? I am not saying you should not put locks on your doors. I am not saying you should not lock your car. I am not saying you should not own a gun, if you believe God has given you permission to own one. That's between you and the Lord. But those things alone will *never* protect you.

Ten thousand could fall at your right hand, but the destruction that got them won't get you, the psalmist says. That's because nothing compares with abiding in the secret place of the Most High. It is the safest place in the world.

LIVING IN THE "NO-HARM" ZONE

In contrast, one of the *least* safest "places" in the world for someone to be is on the receiving end of the wrath of an all-powerful, nobody-can-question-my-decision governmental ruler whom you have totally offended and who, with the snap of his fingers, can have you executed—on the spot, no questions asked. This was the case with three young Jewish men who lived in ancient Babylon under the rule of King Nebuchadnezzar, whose armies had overthrown Israel and subjugated the nation in captivity.

Nebuchadnezzar had made a golden image and decreed that whenever people heard the sound of a certain symphony of music being played they would have to fall down and worship the golden image. (See Daniel 3.) He had said that whoever would not bow would be cast immediately into "a burning fiery furnace." But the three Jews—Shadrach, Meshach and Abed-Nego—would not bow to it.

Literally, they would not play to the world's tune. They would not march to the world's cadence. They would not give themselves over. And Nebuchadnezzar said, in effect, "If you do not bow the knee when you hear that music play, I will ruin you. I will destroy you. I will burn you up. You will have nothing to show for your lives."

"No way. We're not bowing the knee," they said.

Their refusal made Nebuchadnezzar come completely unglued. Now they have totally offended the king—the man who is completely in charge, the man to whom everyone in the country is a subordinate, the man who says, "Do it!" and it gets done.

So he gives the order to fire up the furnace. He is so angry he fires up the furnace seven times hotter than normal. It was so hot that the soldiers who were ordered to put Shadrach, Meshach and Abed-Nego into the fire were burned up while throwing them in.

But for Shadrach, Meshach and Abed-Nego, inside the fire was the safest place on earth for them. They had decided to submit themselves to the mighty hand of God, and that is where God's mighty hand placed them.

When Nebuchadnezzar realized something else was going on in the fire, his reaction is almost comical.

"Didn't we throw three people in that furnace?" he asks those around him.

"Yes, king."

"Well, now there are four in there!"

Most people believe that the fourth man in the fire was none other than the Lord Jesus Christ. I can imagine Shadrach, Meshach and Abed-Nego going, "Man, we're not burning up! Can you believe it? This fire isn't even hot!"

What was happening? They were being protected by the mighty hand of God—so much so that when they came out of the furnace they did not even have the smell of smoke on them.

When you're going through the fire because you have not "bowed the knee," choosing rather to submit yourself under the mighty hand of God, know that God is in there with you.

You will not burn because He is watching over you. When God says that you are not flammable because He is watching over you, then the fire does not touch you.

But who was God standing with in the furnace in Babylon? It was not with wishy-washy believers.

And as far as you and I are concerned today, He does not stand in miraculous ways with people who avoid the fire at any cost—people who say, "I bow the knee to the favor of man and the fear of man. I bow the knee to avoid anything difficult. I bow the knee to pride and an unwillingness to look deep into my life. I bow the knee to not standing with people when things get difficult. I bow the knee to anything that will preserve me and keep me out of the difficult place of honoring God." That kind of wishy-washy living has no place with God.

God stands with people who say, "We will *not* bow the knee to anything that doesn't honor God." I'm not talking about people who are saying they are perfect. Shadrach, Meshach and Abed-Nego were not saying they were perfect. But they did assert that even if God did not deliver them, still they would honor God. So, when they got into the fire, God protected them.

When God says that you are not flammable because He is watching over you, then the fire does not touch you.

As a matter of fact, the only thing in the fire that burned were the ropes that bound them. And so, when you are with God in the fire, not only will it *not* consume you but it will purify you and burn away anything that would seek to bind you from serving the Lord fully.

TAMING THE LIONS

Daniel went through the same kind of thing. He obeyed God at all costs to himself, and God proved Himself—He delivered him. He proved to Daniel that the safest place in the world for him was under His mighty hand.

Daniel had violated an ordinance against prayer, and the law required that he be put to death. It was ordered that he be thrown into a den of lions—even though the king liked Daniel and did not want to put him to death.

> So the king gave the command, and they brought Daniel and cast him into the den of lions. But the king spoke, saying to Daniel, "Your God, whom you serve continually, He will deliver you."
>
> —DANIEL 6:16

Daniel's custom was to pray three times a day. *Daniel was committed to living in Babylon without Babylon living in him.* In order to do that, and to keep his heart pure, he just kept pressing into the Lord. He kept living out Psalm 91—dwelling in the secret place of the Most High, under the shadow of the Almighty, under His wings.

King Darius had already written a decree that if people did not obey his decree, they would be thrown to the lions. He loved Daniel and could not have foreseen the outcome of his decision. But when Daniel violated the decree, Darius realized he had no choice but to put Daniel in with the lions, even though he actually was on Daniel's side and had promoted him and given him authority.

Sometimes when God promotes us, we think, *Well, that's it! No more tests.* But there is always something that will continue to refine our focus and our dependence on the Lord.

Darius told Daniel, "Daniel, your God will be able to deliver you. I don't know everything about this, but I've heard about your God, and He's able to deliver you. The same God that gave you this wisdom is able to deliver you." Isn't it interesting that at times pagans and unbelievers have a clearer view of God than His own people? And sure enough, God shut the lions' mouths and protected Daniel through His mighty hand of protection.

I hear a lot of believers today talking as if the world is nothing but one big lions' den. True, the world is dangerous, *but Jesus said He had overcome the world* (John 16:33). I hear a lot of Christians saying, "Oh, man, I wouldn't want to be a young person growing up in society today."

And I think, *Why not?* I envy some of these young people. What a day to be alive and to be young! What a day to be about the work of the King.

Sure, there are many temptations and many things out there, but none of it takes God by surprise. He knows there is no place safer for us than hidden under His mighty hand of protection.

For you who are parents, do you believe God is able to protect your kids? Why not raise them in the ways of the Lord, showing them something better, something more wonderful, declaring according to Psalm 91 that the plague of rebellion will not come near your dwelling, that the plague of worldliness and carnality will not come near your dwelling and that the plague of young people giving up hope for the future will not come near your dwelling.

Verses 9–10 of Psalm 91 say:

> Because you have made the Lord, who is my refuge, even the Most High, your dwelling place, no evil shall befall you, nor shall any plague come near your dwelling.

This is a verse from God that you need to apply to your own home. Go around your house and speak that no plague is coming near you or near your dwelling and that no evil will befall you or your household. No evil shall befall you when the Lord is your refuge and His mighty hand is your protection.

Passed Over by Danger

Exodus 12 tells about one of the most dramatic examples of God's watching over His people and protecting them. Talk about safety under God's mighty hand.

The chapter marks the beginning of the Passover ritual the Jews were to keep. It describes God's judgment on Pharaoh and Egypt when at midnight He struck dead all the firstborn Egyptians in the land as well as all the firstborn of their livestock.

The plagues came on those who were not God's people—not on God's people. How was it possible to have all those plagues throughout the country, yet in the region where the Israelites lived in slavery there are no plagues? Because when God says no plague will come near your dwelling, that is what He means. God says, "I will protect you," and that's exactly what He means.

Are you abiding in Jesus Christ, the Lamb of God that takes away the sin of the world, and along with it fear of the world? God wants to get us to the point where we understand that He has overcome the world and, because He has, we do not have to fear. God is covering us and protecting us.

Billy Graham Palouse, a young evangelist and missionary I

know, lives on an island off the southern coast of India. He was in America once, leaving his family back home, ministering on the island.

His mother and father called him while he was in America and said to him, "We're just calling to say good-bye."

And he said, "Good-bye? What do you mean?"

"There are marauders coming with swords," they said. "They're coming to kill us. If God doesn't preserve us, we're going to die. So if we do, we'll see you in heaven. Please keep God's work going here." Some of the inhabitants of the island are very much religious radicals who did not have any problem with the idea of killing Billy's parents to protect the sanctity of their own religious way of life.

Billy was very upset and prayed throughout the night, not knowing what would happen to his family. The next day his mom and dad called him, and he was thrilled to hear from them.

"What happened?" he asked.

"When the marauders came to our compound to kill us, we saw angels with flaming swords surrounding them," they answered. "We wondered if just we saw them or if the marauders saw them, too. Then suddenly the marauders looked around and began to scream in terror, running away from us back to their village.

"God then struck them and the whole village with an outbreak of diarrhea that shamed those who came against us and caused many people to come to Christ!"

That is the kind of God we serve. Here were His servants—Billy and his parents—walking in faith and obedience. They were indestructible because God's plan for them was not complete. Thank God, His work for them was far from finished.

As we move on to the next chapter you will discover that the servant of the Lord does not need to fear. God will protect His own.

I WILL NOT BE AFRAID

I will not be afraid of the terror by night;
I will not be afraid of the arrows in flight,
For the shield of your truth is the strength of my life.
Though thousand may fall at my side,
I will not be afraid.

—LYRICS BY DALE EVRIST

Chapter 9

Finding the Place of Protection

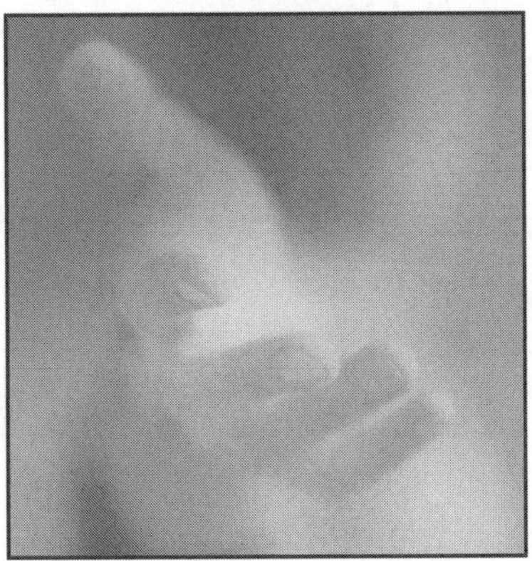

Most of us have an innate desire to find a place of protection. If I am standing in my front yard in the middle of winter with freezing rain coming down, I don't say, "I love nature! It's wonderful!" What do I do? I go inside where I am covered. I put on the heater. I light a fire.

All of us are like that. Whether sitting by a warm fire when it is really cold or finding a cool, shady place in the noonday sun, we all like the feeling of being protected.

Do you enjoy a warm blanket or covers on your bed? Do you get into bed on a chilly night and say, "*Oooh*, I love my bed; I love my pillow." Or do you love to find that shady place in the heat with an ice-cold drink?

We all love that feeling. God is saying to us, "I have something better for you than a blanket or a fireplace in the winter. I have something better for you than a shady place and a cold drink. I have something better for you than a warm, safe home, however wonderful that is.

"Why don't you make your home in My presence? Why don't you come and make your home under My shadow? Why don't you come and let Me wrap My arms of love around you?"

In the Spirit, you feel peace, warmth, nearness and intimacy—because that is what the Spirit is.

The apostle Peter teaches us cast our care on the Lord—all of it—because God loves us and wants us to learn that His mighty hand is greater than all the fears our cares represent.

> Therefore humble yourselves under the mighty hand of God...casting all your care upon Him.
>
> —1 PETER 5:6–7

Care is the breeding ground for fear and anxiety, two emotions that the human psyche is wholly incapable of bearing over the long haul. Fear will paralyze you. Worry will tear you apart. As God's creation, you are not wired to bear the weight of long-term worry and fear. Eventually, they will devastate you.

That's why Jesus said, "Don't worry, you have a heavenly Father who cares for you. If you, being earthly, know how to give good gifts to your children, how much more will your heavenly Father give good things to him who asks?" (See Matthew 6:31; 7:11.)

We have to let God deliver us from "uneven" Christianity. Half the time we are talking faith, and half the time we are talking fear. As a result, we end up spending a lot of time talking out of both sides of our mouths.

I am amazed at how often I can stand in front of our congregation and feel ten feet tall, feel strong in the Lord and talk faith talk. I sound mighty convincing as I encourage myself and our congregation that we are going to live for God every second of every day. Yet how often have I walked down from the platform and gone out into the everyday world and started to whine about my circumstances, wondering what I am going to do. But my commitment, and I hope it's yours too, is to live less and less of an uneven Christian life and more of a fully integrated Christian life where we are trusting God in everything.

I do not want to visit the shadow of the Almighty just a couple of times a week. The Bible says I need to dwell there. When I do, He will be my fortress and my refuge, and in Him I will trust.

In the Spirit, you feel peace, warmth, nearness and intimacy—because that is what the Spirit is.

The hard and difficult things we go through as believers always are filtered through the shadow of the Almighty. God allows only those things that help us to touch us. Even when we feel as if there is an open hunting season sign on us and we are being aimed at from every side, God is our shield, and we do not need to be afraid.

Losing the "Imposter Syndrome"

Have you ever lived through a protracted season in your life in which you had the sense of impending doom? The weight of it hangs over you, hovering over you, and you wonder fretfully when it all is just going to drop on you.

Maybe you live under what I call the "impostor syndrome"—you are sure somebody is going to find out that you do not belong. You think that you are the wrong person to be doing what you are doing. I actually have dreams about somebody standing up in our congregation and saying, "Hey, Dale, why are you up there? You don't know what you're doing."

It isn't that I'm concerned that I *am* an imposter—because I know that God has placed me in the position I am in. The problem is that thoughts come to *accuse* me of not having the right to be in this position.

We do not have to live with this kind of fear.

None of us are ever impostors when we are under the mighty hand of God and carrying out His will for our lives. As long as we know that God has brought us to whatever position we are lifted up to, then when somebody does ask what right we have to be doing what we are doing, we can say, "In and of myself, I don't have a right to be doing anything. But God, by His purpose, has put me in this place. So I am going to make every effort to honor Him and let Him love and communicate some things to you through me."

You see, the point is that you cannot live your life wandering around frightened that what God has called you to do could just end at any moment. God says that you do not have to be afraid of that either. When you are under His mighty hand, He will protect you.

God is the shield that keeps every blow of the enemy from breaking through and breaking you.

There was a time when, as a new father, I would wake up startled and run into my daughter's room and put my hand on her chest just to make sure she was still breathing. One day God said to me, "Do you honestly think that if you had an arsenal of weaponry and every life-saving device in the world in your home that you would have enough power to protect this little girl? You'd better come under the shadow of the Almighty and trust in Me. I'm the only one who has the power to protect your family." At that time, I had a lot of fear in my life. But that word set me free.

Today you may be gripped by the same kind of fear. You will not let your kids out of your sight. What you are really saying to them is, "Kids, if you really want to be safe, abide under my shadow."

But God says, "Wrong. Why don't you bring your whole family under My shadow? I'm the only one who really is able to protect them."

PROTECTED BY HIS TRUTH

Verse 4 of Psalm 91 says, "His truth shall be your shield and buckler."

The apostle Paul gives us instructions about how to withstand the fiery missiles launched at us by Satan:

> Above all, taking the shield of faith with which you will be able to quench all the fiery darts of the wicked one.
>
> —EPHESIANS 6:16

Paul is referring to arrows that have had their tips dipped in pitch, set on fire and then launched from a bow. Roman soldiers who were under attack from arrows of fire carried shields covered in leather. When those arrows came, the soldiers squatted down behind their shields, holding up their shields. As the arrows pierced the shields, immediately they were extinguished because the leather would not burn.

God says that He is a shield for us. He says we do not need to be afraid because of the arrows that fly by day. As the fiery arrows of the devil are sent our way, the Lord covers us. Do you think those fiery missiles harm Him in any way? No way.

He also says He will be a buckler to you. A *buckler* was a small shield designed for use in hand-to-hand combat. The buckler was used in offensive warfare, whereas the large shield was used for defensive warfare.

God is saying that even when you are in the fiercest battle, when you are in an offensive rather than defensive mode, He is your buckler. He is the shield that keeps all of your vital organs protected. God is the shield that keeps every blow of the enemy from breaking through and breaking you.

God's truth shall be your shield and buckler, shielding you from harm. The truth of His Word, the truth of His prophetic promise over your life, will shield you from all harm. When the enemy comes against you, especially as a New Testament believer, with his weapons of choice—lies, bluffs and deception—you counteract him with the truth.

How do we withstand the attacks of the enemy? We withstand by the truth of God's Word. Humbling ourselves under the mighty hand of God presupposes that we are coming under the biblical standard for truth and that we are committed to letting His Word be our shield and defense.

Protected by His Light

One thing the enemy tries to do is to play on our fears about the unknown. But the Lord says, "You shall not be afraid of the terror by night" (Ps. 91:5).

You do not need to be afraid of things that threaten you, the things that play on your fears as you lie in bed at night—things you may have no control over. You can lie down at night and sleep, knowing that you do not have to be afraid of the terror by night.

"But they're attacking me, Lord!" you say.

"Don't be afraid."

"They're lying about me, God."

"I've got this one."

"They're ruining my reputation."

"Well, I became of *no* reputation. Why don't you try that? I've got you covered."

God says we do not need to be afraid of "the pestilence that walks in darkness"—the sense that "there's something out there, and it's going to get me." So many of us live with fear. Maybe we think we are exerting due caution by allowing ourselves to live within the boundaries of our fears.

That's not what God says. He says we do not need to be afraid, even when we are thinking the worst about a situation.

One day not long ago I was having chest pains. I had entered my forties, and *boom!* All of a sudden I have the pains, which of course were immediately followed by the thought, *Maybe it's my heart.* I didn't know what to attribute it to, but I was tempted to think the worst. When I made an appointment with my internist, I was put through a series of tests—the treadmill test, an EKG and others.

"Well, Mr. Evrist," the doctor said, "whatever is causing these pains, it has nothing to do with your heart. But I know how easy it is to let your mind tell you that it is. I'm a doctor, and we are the biggest hypochondriacs in the world. When something is wrong with me, I don't diagnosis myself and assume there's nothing wrong with me. I get with my professional friends, and say: 'Check me! Check me!'"

That examination with the doctor led me to the best diagnosis I ever received—I needed to check with God! I needed to get a sense of whether or not He was finished with His plan for my life! When He assured me that He had more for me to do, I realized again that as I walked in faith and obedience, God's hand would continue to protect me and lead me into the future.

Protected Because We Are His

In verses 7–8 of Psalm 91, God basically is telling us, "I know it's a weird world that you live in. I know there are a lot of strange and threatening things, but don't you know that I make a distinction between My people and those who are not My people? Don't you know that you are not like everybody else in the world if you are *My* people?"

> A thousand may fall at your side, and ten thousand at your right hand; but it shall not come near you. Only with your eyes shall you look, and see the reward of the wicked.

Think about that, parents. You distinguish between your kids and other people's kids. And for good reason. That's because your children are your responsibility. In the same way, because we are God's children *we are God's responsibility*. And His hand of protection is extended to us because we are His.

Verse 6 of Psalm 91 says we do not have to fear "the destruction that lays waste at noonday." We do not have to be afraid of destruction in daylight—things that can come unexpectedly upon any of us.

Sometimes these attacks come in the form of temptation. You walk out into the light of day, and you feel vulnerable; you feel open to the attacks. But God says, "If you will abide in Me, I will be a shield for you. When those arrows fly, I will extinguish them."

"A thousand may fall at your side," verse 7 says—or ten thousand—but it will not come near you. It isn't that God does not love other people. And it isn't that God in His sovereignty does not preserve the lives of people who will later come to Him.

We are God's responsibility.

But you need to know that as a child of God you have a place in God because you belong to Him. You have the privilege of calling upon God's hand of protection. God will preserve you through the most challenging and difficult things, sparing you through times when not only will you live and not die, *but you will thrive* because God's mighty hand has watched over you.

Protected by Heaven's Bodyguards

Psalm 91:11–12 adds a whole new element to the explanation of God's protection:

> For He shall give His angels charge over you, to keep you in all your ways. In their hands they shall bear you up, lest you dash your foot against a stone.

Verse 11 tells us that the shadow of the Almighty comes with angels—and it doesn't mean the little ornamental ones from the Christian bookstore that you pin on your lapel. This verse is talking about angels of protection—the big, burly ones.

"He shall give His angels charge over you." They are ordered to keep watch over you when you abide in the secret place of the Most High. When you come under God's mighty hand, God orders His angels over you. As they take their positions of watchfulness over you, He tells them, "Protect them. Cover them. They've submitted themselves to Me. They are under Me. Watch over them. Watch over their children, watch over their belongings."

This was the kind of protection a couple in our church experienced one Christmas. God had recently done a miraculous work in healing this couple's marriage, and they were happily anticipating an exciting Christmas together. The healing of this couple's marriage had come after a long and protracted time of separation that lasted over six months. Both had submitted themselves to come under the mighty hand of God, believing that the healing in their marriage was according to His prophetic assignment. They had also submitted themselves to leadership and to the counsel of trusted friends, knowing that their only hope was to live in proper alignment. During this time of separation, they experienced frustration, pain, many tears and the need to forgive hurts. At times it looked as though their marriage would not make it. But as they submitted themselves to the Lord and to the process, they received the product, which was a healed marriage.

On this particular Christmas morning the family gathered around the Christmas tree to open gifts. As they opened their gifts, a fire broke out in their home. Sparks from the fireplace headed up to the chimney and ignited some flammable objects in the attic, and they began to smell smoke. They were able to get the entire family out to safety before anyone was harmed. But although everyone was spared because of the miraculous protection of God, they lost their home and everything in it.

God later restored to this couple everything they lost in the fire. Even when it seems that you literally or figuratively have gone through the fire, God is able to protect you. Just as He was with Shadrach, Meshach and Abed-Nego—and with this couple—He will be with and will preserve you and yours.

If, in the spiritual dimension, we could only see those angels of protection who are watching over us. What do they look like? How tall are they? How massive are their muscles? What do they wear? What are their names? Only eternity will reveal how many of us have gone to bed at night with ministering angels of fire standing on the perimeter of our property as sentries keeping watch over us because God has ordered their protection over us. If we only knew how many times things could have been so much worse had God not protected us...how many times things would have happened to us but did not because God protected us.

PROTECTED BY HIS PEACE

When you were a child, if you lived in any semblance of a healthy home, you did not go to bed at night saying, "Oh, man! What if I don't make it until tomorrow?" You just went to bed.

Can you imagine hearing a conversation like the following?

"Mommy?"

"Yes, honey, what is it?"

"I've been thinking about our finances. Are you sure you and Dad have really thought through the whole thing of planning for tomorrow? Can I see the checkbook again? I'd just like to go over a couple of figures before I go to sleep."

"Honey, you're four years old. What are you talking about?"

Have you ever heard a young child talk like that when he is drifting off to sleep? No, children just go to sleep, don't they?

I grew up as a church kid, and I remember being carried to the car like a sack of potatoes over my dad's shoulder as we went to the car to leave church after a long service. My dad would carry me over his right shoulder and my brother over his left shoulder as he walked out to the car.

I can remember that "lifeless" feeling—you know, you're sort of drooling all the way to the car, but you don't care. You feel safe, and that is what counts. As my dad laid us on the back seat of the car we would drift off to sleep.

I did not lie there in the car thinking, *Gee, I hope Dad's had enough sleep. I hope he's going to be OK. You know, there are a lot of crazies out there.* I did not think about that when I was five years old. I just went to sleep in the car.

But when you get older, you start thinking about all the things that can go wrong. Yet God says that if we will come under His hand of protection, we will not have to worry.

If you and I only realized what we are capable of as we trust in God's powerful hand of protection. If we only realized what situations we are capable of walking through. You might be saying, "I can't make it!"

You can make it. Is God with you?

"Yes."

Has God called you to this?

"Yes."

You can make it. He will protect you through it.

Others of you might be saying, "But I don't want to stay in this marriage—my heart is breaking."

God will protect your heart and your mind in Christ Jesus. That's what the Bible says. He will guard your heart and your mind in Christ Jesus (Phil. 4:7).

You are facing extreme difficulties: "This is frightening; I've never been in this level of spiritual warfare before."

God has. He has been there before, and He is not afraid. Remember, He is your shield and your buckler, so you do not have to be afraid.

Perhaps you are afraid of the unknown: "I don't know what the future holds."

God does.

Maybe you are wounded: "Something happened in my life that was traumatic, and I'm afraid to trust again."

Well, just know that the best place to rebuild trust and to repair your broken world is to come back under the strong hand of God's care and protection.

In the secret place of the Most High, under the shadow of the Almighty, under His wings is your refuge. He is your fortress, your God, in Him you can trust. God will lead you. God will guide you.

Delivered by Devotion

Psalm 91:14–15 says, "Because he has set his love upon me, therefore I will deliver him. I will set him on high"—that means to pull out of trouble. "I will answer him"—there's a response and a remedy when you call upon the Lord. "I will be with him in trouble"—God will be by your side in difficult times.

Recently my wife and I went through the most challenging year of our lives in ministry. We dealt with assault and accusations that were more severe than anything we had ever known before. We had dealt with criticism, as anyone will in ministry—some of it fair, some of it unfair. But this was different. Many of the things that were being said were just simply outrageous. Much of it we knew was, in one way or another, demonically inspired to try to discourage us and drive us from the very calling to ministry that God had made so clear to us many, many times.

It wasn't that we did not have things to learn in this season. It was just that in this season of learning, the enemy was attempting to destroy us. The fire had been stoked, the heat was turned up and the enemy had our destruction in mind.

But what we discovered was that when the heat is turned up, God draws nearer and nearer to us. We had never sensed the Lord closer to us than we did in that season of difficulty, and God brought us through unsinged and unwavering in our devotion to serve Him.

That is why Jesus came into Nebuchadnezzar's fire. He came into the fire as an illustration that when the fire is turned up seven times hotter than normal, He is in there saying to you, "Feel the cool breeze. Feel the cool breeze of my Spirit."

There is not one ounce of wasted material in the trials God takes us through. And the difficulties He allows for us are never about destroying us. They are always about helping us. God wants us to run to Him for refuge because if we are under the mighty hand of God, then those trials that are filtered through the shadow of the Almighty—even when they touch us and cause us pain—are for our healing and for our strengthening.

The best place to rebuild trust and to repair your broken world is to come back under the strong hand of God's care and protection.

God is able to deliver you if you will trust Him.

Verses 15–16 of Psalm 91 say, "I will deliver him and honor him"—that's rescue and reward. "With long life I will satisfy him." And so we need to trust God that with long life He will satisfy us, and that He will show us His salvation so that we may take His salvation to others who need it.

Drink deeply of His deliverance. Learn what it means to have God rescue you time and time again. In doing so you will know for yourself and be able to point others to the fact that God's mighty hand is a hand of protection.

Fight On

Though you grow tired and ready to surrender,
There's One who's gone before, and He has won the war.
So come lay down your weakness,
And you will find His strength is more.

Fight on,
Though the battle rages long.
Fight on,
For our Savior's power is strong.
Fight on,
And sorrow's pain will soon give way to victory's song.
Fight on.

—Lyrics by Dale Evrist and Michael O'Brien

Chapter 10

A Hand of Power

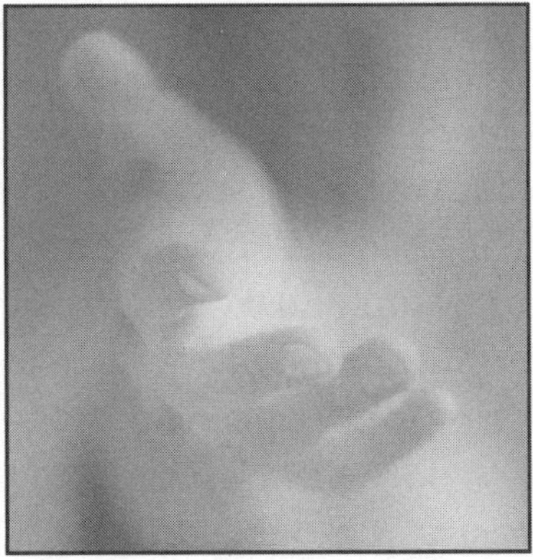

Greg and Lisa's infant son, Blake, was diagnosed with a medical condition in which two of the four growth plates of his skull grew together before his brain finished maturing. Usually a child's brain has finished growing by about age two, and the boney growth plates fuse together to finish forming the skull.

Two of Blake's growth plates had fused together in the womb, and as his brain continued to grow it caused his head to elongate, resembling the shape of a football. Even though Greg and Lisa's doctors initially believed that in time Blake's head would reshape itself properly, it was later discovered that Blake was the one in about two thousand babies whose head would not reshape itself. He would require plastic surgery to be made normal.

Devastated, Greg and Lisa researched their son's condition and prayed that God would heal Blake in the way that would bring Him the most glory. They prayed to be directed to the right physicians and medical staff. They researched the surgeon whom they had been referred to. They discovered that he was a leading specialist in this particular field of surgery and that he practiced at a children's hospital only twenty minutes from their home.

Upon examining Blake, the physician told Greg and Lisa that correcting their son's condition would involve eight hours of surgery, a blood transfusion, a four-day stay in the pediatric intensive care unit, three more days in a private room at the hospital and an eight-week recovery at home. Again, Greg and Lisa were devastated. They had not realized how serious the procedure was for correcting Blake's condition. Because the Thanksgiving and Christmas season was approaching, Greg and Lisa made plans to have Blake operated on before the holidays.

Less than a week before Blake's scheduled surgery, Greg and Lisa learned their surgeon needed to have emergency back surgery and that Blake's operation would have to be postponed for eight weeks. Despite the shock and disappointment, they stood in faith that God's hand was on each person's schedule who was related to the surgery and also on the medical staff who would be performing the operation.

After the holidays, Greg and Lisa quickly picked up where they had left off with preparations for Blake's operation. The day before his surgery, a man from our church, David, asked to speak with them. He told them that while he had been praying for Blake, he had a vision of Blake's surgery. He gave the couple a sketch he had drawn after he had the vision. It was a pencil sketch of the surgical team in the operating room, and it included the equipment, lights and various medical instruments on the table.

The detail of the artwork was incredible. Blake lay on the operating table with a peaceful look on his face as he slept. His head was perfectly shaped and being cradled in the hands of Jesus, who was standing at the head of the table overseeing the work of the doctors and nurses. The drawing of Blake's face and head looked just like him, even though David had never seen Blake.

As Greg and Lisa looked at that sketch and listened to the man describe his vision, they were filled with an awesome sense of the power God had to transform a difficult situation of life and replace anxiousness and uncertainty with His peace. They prepared for Blake's surgery the next day with a newly deepened sense of peace and confidence.

The expected eight-hour surgery took only four hours, a confirmation for Greg and Lisa that Jesus was there in the operating room giving the doctors and nurses His power to perform the operation. As Greg and Lisa waited for news of Blake's progress, they remembered that drawing of Blake's head cradled in the mighty hands of Jesus.

Blake spent only five days in the hospital instead of the eight that had been planned. Within three weeks after Blake came home from the hospital, life for Greg and Lisa was pretty much back to normal. Even though they had been concerned that the trauma of an extensive surgery could have a lasting effect on Blake's joyful, easygoing disposition, it didn't—and hasn't. Blake is considered to be fully healed from his condition.

Greg and Lisa went through one of life's biggest tests for a parent—a threat to the physical safety and security of their child—and learned that God's power was able to overshadow even the most trying circumstance of their life at a time when they themselves were powerless.

That is a fact—and God wants all of us to know it applies to our lives as well.

His Power Is Able to Set Us Free

It is when we are powerless that God's power works best on our behalf. Greg and Lisa learned that as they saw God physically heal their son through the skills of the medical staff that He chose for them.

In the same way, God's power becomes strong on our behalf when the nature of our problem is spiritual. Whether we wrestle with something that is greater than us in a physical or spiritual nature, it is when we are powerless to help ourselves that God often will work His greatest miracles for us through *His* power.

A friend once told me a story about a demon-possessed woman who had started coming to his church. He was a youth pastor, just a young minister, and he did not have much experience in prevailing prayer. He did not know the Word as well as he would have liked, nor did he know a lot about walking in the power of God.

He and others in his church were doing the best they could to minister to this woman, who was utterly demonized. All of their efforts, however, had been futile. They could not physically restrain her long enough to minister to her. Because the demons within her had supernatural strength, the woman was able to fling my friend and anyone else away from her when they tried to approach her for ministry.

After numerous unsuccessful attempts to set her free, they were at a loss for what to do. They were all inexperienced with deliverance, so they called on the more seasoned senior pastor, pleading for his help. In response to their call, he drove over to the church while the woman was there.

As he turned into the parking lot of the church, the woman began to scream, "Keep him away from me!" No one in my friend's group had seen the pastor drive up, and there weren't any new persons among them, so they asked her, "Who? Who? Keep who away from you?"

"Him! The one who's coming!" she shrieked.

With that, the seasoned pastor entered the church building, then came into the room where they were waiting. He walked up to the woman, took her and wrapped her tightly in his arms, and then spoke into her ear, "In the name of Jesus, loose her!"

She crumpled immediately to the ground, set free that instant by the power of God. My friend and the others stood there rather sheepishly, thinking, *Oh. Why didn't we try that?*

I think all of us as believers can relate to that story because we have had times in our lives, and perhaps are still living in times, where we have not come to terms with what it means to access and release the power of God to heal and deliver.

My friend and the others certainly could have spoken in the name of Jesus to release God's power into the situation. But they did not know quite how to do so. Their seasoned pastor, however, knew about the awesome power in the name of Jesus.

He had learned what the Bible says about the mighty hand of God—that it is a hand of power that will raise from the dead, deliver from darkness, heal from sin and sickness, save eternally and give us peace. Ephesians 1:18–22 says:

> [I pray that] the eyes of your understanding being enlightened; that you may know what is the hope of His calling, what are the riches of the glory of His inheritance in the saints, and what is the exceeding greatness of His power toward us who believe, according to the working of His mighty power which He worked in Christ when He raised Him from the dead and seated Him at His right hand in the heavenly places, far above all principality and power and might and dominion . . . and . . . put all things under His feet.

You can bet that because God says He wants you to know "what is the exceeding greatness of His power toward us who believe," the devil is running scared and wants to make sure that you are clueless about the power you have in Jesus Christ. The power that *you* have in Christ.

The mighty hand of God is more powerful than Satan—the great oppressor of mankind. And the power and authority to defeat Satan and his demons belong to the believer. Like Jesus, we have the power to see Satan crushed under our feet. According to Romans 16:20, we find that the Word says, "And the God of peace will crush Satan under your feet shortly. The grace of our Lord Jesus Christ be with you. Amen." When confronted with God's mighty hand of power Satan has no choice but to crumple to the ground in defeat.

The way to activate your weapon is by knowing, believing and speaking what the Bible says about you.

Because of the cross, Satan's power is reduced to the strength of a squirt gun when he faces the resurrection power of Jesus Christ. If you are a Christian, know that God has placed the spiritual equivalent of an assault rifle in your hands. Yet the devil has managed to convince so many of us that he remains stronger than we are and can attack us, tempt us and defeat us whenever he would like.

Even though God has placed a powerful weapon in your hands, it does you no good if you do not take the safety off and fire it at the enemy. The way to activate your weapon is by knowing, believing and speaking what the Bible says about you. The Word of God in your heart and in your mouth is your ammunition, and it is all-important that you fill your heart and your mouth with God's Word.

In today's world there are many people who need to experience the powerful hand of God raised in authority against Satan. Our cities are filled with men and women who have fallen prey to the enemy and his oppressive tactics to bind the lives of men and women in bondage to him. Even many Christians live powerless, impotent lives, unable to defeat Satan and his oppressions against them. Remember, it does you no good if you do not take the safety off your spiritual weapon and fire it at the enemy. Live in the power and authority of your mighty God—and share that power with those who need it most.

Ordinary People Who Serve an Extraordinary God

The twelve disciples were just normal guys. They were not a group of polished theologians. The Scripture shows us a bunch of guys standing around talking when Jesus said, "Guys, come here!"

"Yes, sir?"

These are twelve uneducated Galileans. These guys, like so many of us, are one word away from saying something *really foolish*.

"Who do men say that I am?" Jesus asked Simon Peter.

"You are the Christ, the Son of the living God!"

"Good one, Peter! Flesh and blood did not reveal that to you, but My Father who's in heaven did."

So Peter struts his stuff around the other twelve: "Yeah, You're the Christ, the Son of the living God. Just call me Prophet Peter."

Then Jesus began to tell them that He has to go to Jerusalem and suffer many things at the hands of the scribes and Pharisees. Peter says, "Fellows, back off. I need to straighten the Lord out."

"Jesus," Peter says, "these things will never happen to you."

He is waiting for Jesus to say, "Ah, Peter! Thank you!"

But Jesus turns instead and says, "Get behind me, Satan! You aren't thinking the things of God; you're thinking about the things of man."

Satan?! Peter wondered. *What happened to flesh and blood didn't reveal this to me?*

You see, this Peter who would one day be a pillar among God's people was a *pillar in process.* He was not perfect. And neither were the rest of the disciples. They grew as we grow, and they got better and better. But Jesus took these imperfect men and called them together and said, "I'm going to give you power and authority. Power *and* authority."

That's the same power and authority that you and I have today.

Luke 9:1 says, "Then He called His twelve disciples together and gave them power and authority over *all* demons" (emphasis added).

Over how many demons did He give them authority? *All.* Over every last one of them.

Can you imagine Jesus calling you aside and saying, "I'm giving you authority over every demonic force that is out there?" You think that might charge you with a little bit of confidence? These disciples have already seen Jesus whip the devil from every angle, and now He is saying, "I'm giving *you* that same authority."

What do you think happens when your name comes up in hell? Do the demons quake with fear, or do they shake with laughter?

In Matthew 28:18–19 Jesus proclaimed, "All authority has been given to Me in heaven and on earth. Go therefore, and make disciples of all the nations."

And we know from Mark 16 that He declared, "Go preach the gospel. Cast out demons, heal the sick. People are going to speak with new tongues. All heaven is going to break loose—I've given you the authority" (vv. 15–18, paraphrased).

Acts 1:8 sends us out in that power and authority: "But you shall receive power when the Holy Spirit has come upon you; and you shall be witnesses to Me in Jerusalem, and in all Judea and Samaria, and to the end of the earth."

God has given His followers a supernatural authority that we need to put into action. It is our inheritance as God's children. It is an authority and power that was first given to Adam in the Garden of Eden. But that power and authority were lost when man sinned. Satan wrenched it out of man's hands and became the ruler of the earth. But when Jesus died on the cross of Calvary He took that power and authority away from the devil and gave it back to His followers. When we operate in God's power and authority, we are armed and ready to exercise authority over all the demonic powers of this world—including over Satan himself. Our warfare weapons thwart the very gates, or councils, of hell.

Do you walk in God's power enough to threaten hell? What do you think happens when your name comes up in hell? Do the demons quake with fear, or do they shake with laughter?

If my name comes up in hell, do demons say, "*Aw*, you don't have to worry about him. Are you kidding—he's no threat to us. He's scared of his own shadow."

Or do they say, "We've got to do something about this guy. He really believes in the Word of God and the power of God. He's a threat to us."

Do you want to be a threat to the devil? Do you want the demons to shriek in terror and not roll with laughter at the sound of your name? If you need a greater conviction about this, the mighty hand of God will help you. You *have* the power.

Confessions of a Defeated Foe

When God raised Christ from the dead, He placed Him over all spiritual rulers, leaders and authorities. That's why you get such a reaction when you bring up the name of Jesus. It is the name above every name. Demons that scream with rage scream with terror when you say, "In Jesus' name!"

Because of Jesus' death on the cross and resurrection from the dead, Satan is a defeated foe. God stripped him of his power over us while putting Jesus at His own "right hand," meaning that God's power and authority is in Jesus.

In the 1980s there was a popular song by Christian music artist Carman titled "The Champion." It used a dramatic lyrical style to narrate the story of how God powerfully triumphed over Satan. In those days, a lot of Christians were adapting its lyrical content and message to create dramatic evangelistic performances.

Around that time I was in England leading a music and drama team, and we were doing our own version of "The

Champion." Our team was decked out in costume and painted up with very scary, really wild makeup.

Somehow I got cast in the role of Satan. (That was a little unnerving for some of my church members at the time!) The ministry we were doing was very effective, and a lot of people were coming to Christ, due in part to this drama.

The key scene in our drama was the climactic fight in which I, as Satan, got the daylights kicked out of me by Jesus to the cheers of everyone in the audience. At the end of that scene an evangelist who traveled with us would come on stage to preach and call people to give their lives to Jesus.

One Sunday morning at a certain church in England, I found out our evangelist was scheduled to speak at another service, and I was left to preach after the big fight scene. But at the end of that scene I was lying lifeless on the ground, which I did not think was the best time to get up and try to preach the gospel, especially for someone playing Satan. Besides, I did not think the impact would be as effective for the audience if my character did the preaching. But I also knew there was no time for me to get out of costume and makeup, change my clothes and then come back out to preach.

While praying about how to handle this, I thought I heard the Lord say, "Preach as Satan. Preach in character as Satan." I had never done that before, and I have never done it since.

But I sensed that God was up to something with this and that He would use it effectively in the lives of those in the congregation. So when the time came, there I was, lain out on the stage before the congregation after being defeated by the power of God. I could hear people in the audience saying, "Oh, dear, what's he doing there? Why doesn't he get up? He's just lying there—it's rather strange."

Slowly I began to rise. I had full makeup and costume on. I began to walk toward them, and they were saying, "Oh, dear. Here he comes. In the name of Jesus, get out of here!" They were taking it pretty seriously, which was good, because at least I had their attention.

Then I began to preach a message called "Confessions of a Defeated Foe." I confessed to them that I was utterly defeated, that I had no power over believers' lives, that I was doomed for hell and that I was going to try to take as many people with me as I could.

I also told them that as long as I was defeated, I was going to do everything in my power to cause people to believe that I was *not* defeated. I would do whatever it would take to convince people that I had power over their lives and that they could never get right with God. After all, Jesus called Satan the Father of Lies, and God had told me to preach in character.

While I was doing this—walking among the congregation and preaching—I stopped next to a woman. I did not know her or her situation. I would find out later that this woman was the biggest gossip in the church, always criticizing everyone, always tearing down the leadership with her words. But at the time, I did not have a clue about that.

Unaware of the impact my words were having on her, I looked her in the eyes and said—as Satan, "When you gossip about other believers and criticize leadership in a cruel manner, thank you." I took her hand and said, "We're in the ministry together."

Some Christians actually are more of a threat to the church than to the devil because they have unwittingly aligned themselves with the devil. Some Christians live to criticize and accuse other Christians. But the Bible is very clear about who the accuser of the church is (or should be!), and that is Satan.

Later, I was told that this woman had repented after that. She knew there was no way I could have known that what I had said was actually true of her.

We need to understand that Jesus has utterly defeated Satan. The mighty hand of God is a hand of power that raised Jesus from the dead, triumphed over the devil and all of hell and rules over all of God's enemies and ours.

You and I have the seal of the Holy Spirit. We are not just renegade warriors. We are delegates of a king from another kingdom who says, "Go and use My power to defeat all of hell and all of darkness."

God's ultimate triumph was the victory He wrought in Christ over the grave. He has the power over demonic darkness—over all demons—so that we no longer need to be afraid. We can say to our children, "You don't need to be afraid of the devil. You don't need to go to bed at night and be afraid. Just call us and say, 'Come and pray with me.'" We can teach our children that anytime anything tries to come against them, they only have to say, "In the name of Jesus I'm safe. In the name of Jesus I'm free. In the name of Jesus I'm protected." We will find that if this powerful truth gets into our kids, it will be a great reminder for us as parents, too.

God's mighty hand has power over all demons, and we need not fear them.

KnowGodNoFear.calm

In this computer age most of us are familiar with websites and website addresses where we can log on to get various information and goods. Well, I would like to let you know that there is a site that we may call KnowGodNoFear.calm, which is not an earthly website but a heavenly website to which you and I can log on at any time through faith-filled prayer.

Some people will discourage you, though—sometimes unknowingly, sometimes intentionally—in believing that because of some things that have happened in your life this kind of fear and calm is not available to you by saying, "Well, you've made your bed; now lie in it." That is another way of saying that if we have messed up in our lives we have no choice but to live fully with the consequences of bad choices.

But that is not what God says.

He says, "Even if you dug the grave and then lay down in it, come forth! I am greater than any of your mistakes. I am greater than any of your failures. I am greater than any of your regrets. I am greater than any of the shameful things that have been done by you, to you or any of the things that have been said about you. Like Lazarus of old, get those grave clothes off and come forth into the fullness of new life!"

Maybe you are saying, "Well, that's easy for you to say, Dale. You've been to Bible college. You're an ordained minister. The devil is sure to listen to you, but what about me?"

It does not matter.

The smallest child filled with the power of God can cause the biggest demon to shriek with terror when God comes to lay His hand of power on that young person. I know a little girl like that in our congregation. Her name is Hannah. Not long ago, I told my congregation, "This little girl filled with the power of God isn't just Hannah, she's 'Hurricane Hannah.'" You know what Hannah did when she heard that? She decided to "change" her name because she believed that was her true identity. She informed her mom and dad, "I want to change my name." (Some people called her "Hannah Banana.") She said, "I don't want to be Hannah Banana anymore. I like what Pastor Dale said. Call me Hurricane Hannah. I love that!"

The smallest child who is filled with the power of God is a direct threat to the devil. One teenager who is passionate for God and wants to walk in power is a direct threat to the devil. An elderly person who is experiencing the diminished capacities that can come with old age is every bit as powerful in the Spirit as when younger—even though the outward man may be perishing. Still the inward man is renewed day by day (2 Cor. 4:16).

Let me encourage you—laugh in the devil's face, even if he roars at you.

If he shouts, "I'm going to kill you," answer back, "No, you're not! I'm indestructible until God's plan for me is complete."

When he says, "Your ministry's over," put him in his place and say, "No, *you're* over, devil."

When he mocks, "I warn you, I'll continually remind you of your past," give it right back and say, "I warn you, I'll continually remind you of your future."

When he threatens, "I know where you come from," remind him of the truth, "Well, Jesus has cleansed me of all that, and I know where you're going. And it's not to heaven."

When Satan says to you that you have no choice but to sin, you can say to him, "No. *You* have no choice but to go. I take authority over you by the mighty power of God." Also remember this, we are in a battle, and sometimes when we resist, Satan will insist. But if we will persist, he has to go.

By Jesus' authority, sin no longer dominates us. Instead, we learn to dominate sin. We learn to bring sin under subjection instead of sin bringing us under subjection.

Satan's key weapon against you is to convince you to believe a lie—to believe that he is not defeated and that he still has power over your life. If he can get you to believe that, you are under his feet, instead of the reverse being true. When you are under his feet he will try to link you with his schemes, which is what he had done with that woman in England.

Remember, a lie has power only if you believe it. The truth has power only if you believe it. So choose the truth and reject the lie.

The enemy hates the church. He wants to assail the church, defeat the church, even destroy the church—although we are reminded of Jesus' words that He would build His church and the gates of hell would not be able to destroy it (Matt. 16:18). Still, when we link with the enemy, we can just watch God's power factor drop in our lives.

Satan knows he cannot take you to hell. So he will try to throw as much of hell at you as he can. He will try to get you to link with hell as much as he can so he can dilute you, drain the power of God from your life, neutralize you and render you ineffective for the cause of Christ and the Great Commission.

But God does not want us to have anything to do with that. God, through His mighty hand of power, can make you laugh in the face of fear. He wants you to be touched by His power and to take that power and touch a suffering world.

A lie has power only if you believe it. The truth has power only if you believe it.

One of the greatest fears that we face is the fear of failure. But when we really come to understand what it means to live by prophetic assignment and in proper alignment, and we are going forth according to the will of God for our lives, it is God's mighty hand of power that will enable us to fulfill everything He has called us to do. We do not need to fear failure, because we live under the authority of the One who has triumphed over everything.

You Can Be Freed From the Fear of Man

Some of us are so worried about the opinions of man. We are more worried about what people think about us than what God thinks about us.

"What are they thinking? What if they don't like me? What if they say mean things about me?" we ask. "What if I'm fired from my job? What will I do? Where will I go? What if my spouse leaves me and takes the children?"

Well, you will live and not die because God loves you. God, in fact, thinks you are wonderful.

"Yeah, but they think I'm stupid."

So they are wrong.

"They say I'm never going to make it."

So they are wrong.

"They say I'm going to be destroyed—be a total failure."

So they are wrong.

Oh, it's true that the devil sometimes will try to use people who will say things to you like, "I will ruin you!" But your mind-set and my mind-set need to be, "No, you won't. But you will ruin yourself if you don't stop saying things like that."

Can you get hold of that?

What can man do to you? If God is for you, who can be against you? How can the opinions of others ultimately stop you if God is behind you, if His power is opening a door for you or making a way for you? (See Romans 8:31–39.)

In Proverbs 29:25 the Bible says that the fear of man is a snare. When we fear other people or their opinions about us, and we allow that fear to paralyze us, then we have, in effect, allowed ourselves to be snared by their opinions of us. Consenting to the negative things people say about us instead of believing and acting on what God says about us traps us within their opinions. It limits how much of God's power can effectively work through us.

It is amazing that those of us who live in a Western culture are far too concerned about image. That's a big deal in the city that I live in. Oftentimes people are tempted to cop an attitude of needing to look just a little bit too cool for the room.

In some ways, image can be everything. How are we perceived? What are we projecting? What is it that we need to be projecting? What does the market demand? What are people wanting? All of these things can cause us to bend our whole lives so that we will be perceived as cool or hip or desirable by others, rather than simply being the person that God has called us to be. This is one of the ways that we can walk in the fear of man. Stop trying to be what man wants you to be, and start being the best that God has called you to be. And it is the power of God that will deliver you from the need to try to project an image that will be pleasing to man, and in some cases, will ultimately not be pleasing to God.

We need to live from a platform of conviction that has been borne out of our study of the Word of God and the inner witness of the Spirit of God. The Word teaches us not to fear man: "The fear of man brings a snare, but whoever trusts in the Lord shall be safe" (Prov. 29:25). We all need to share what we believe without the fear of man, while always being ready to be corrected and adjusted. But we should never shrink back from opportunities to share what we believe to be the truth because we fear man's response.

When I stand before my congregation, I have to convey what God has put in my heart to say in a way that fits my personality. God does not expect me to be like some other famous, well-known preacher. He does not want me to be anyone but the person He created me to be. When I am standing for the truth, some of the things that I say might cause someone initially to be upset with me. Sometimes people will come up to me and say, "That thing you said last week really made me mad."

To which I might reply, "Really? What was it?"

I ask that because sometimes I might have said something untrue or insensitive for which I need to repent. But if the person's response is that he or she was angry about something I said that is a clearly taught truth in the Word of God, then I will want to know, "Well, what did you do about it?"

And I am really encouraged if they answer, "I went home, got out my Bible, started looking and found out that you were right. God really convicted me, and I am letting Him make the changes in my life that need to be made."

The fear of man can keep the follower of God bound in mediocre Christian living. But, as the Word promises, if we trust in the Lord we can overcome our fear of man and live in the power and authority Christ purchased for us at the cross of Calvary. I am telling you this for one reason: Let God's mighty hand of power touch you, and all of a sudden you will find your backbone is strong—not with arrogance, but with serene confidence that is born out of a sense of God's will for your life, His love for you, the gifts He has placed in your life and the value that those gifts have when released in humble ministry into the lives of others.

What difference does it make what man can do? God is for you. No one can be against you when God is on your side. *No one.*

Mighty Love

I'm learning to let love in;
With boldness now I'm drawing near,
Letting Your passion flood my heart,
Casting out all of my fear,
Confident faith, confident faith now is rising.
And I know that it's all because
You've broken through my sorrow and tears
By the power of Your mighty love.

Your mighty love is healing me;
Your mighty love makes my doubts flee.
Your mighty love has set me free;
It's a mighty, mighty love.

—Lyrics by Dale Evrist

Chapter 11

Plugging In to God's Power Surge

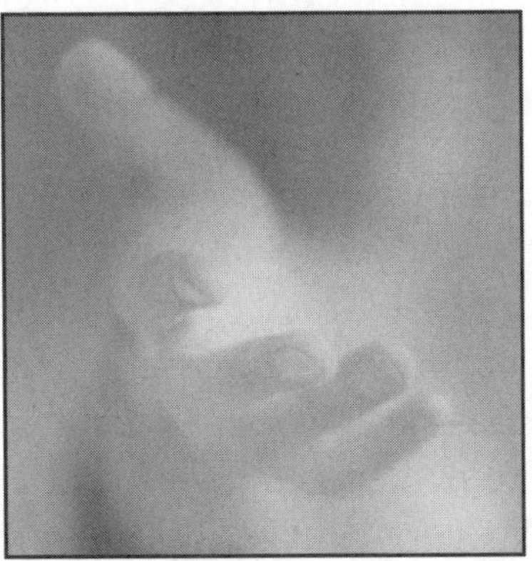

Like lots of things in life, the power that exists in God is "better felt than telt." When we come into direct contact with an awesome display of the mighty power of God, it is a lot easier to trust Him to come through for us in difficult times.

Most of us have seen a *Superman* movie. It was pretty hard for us to believe that kind, sweet-tempered Clark Kent could do anything to right the injustices of life. But watching that transformation in the phone booth to Superman and seeing him demonstrate his mighty powers gave us hope that the wrongs would be made right.

Most every school child could tell you the secret to Superman's strength. It lay in heritage—he was not born of earth; he was "superborn," the offspring of a powerful super race from outer space.

But Superman was a wimp compared to our mighty God. And the power of God transcends any power on earth—or in space. There are three great words in the Greek language that I love that are used to define our word *power*. Each of these terms is crucial to our understanding of the power in the mighty hand of God. They are:

- *Kratos*—"manifested power to rule over everything"
- *Exousia*—"the legal right to rule on another's behalf"
- *Dunamis*—"power expressed with visible results"

Taken together, these terms exemplify God's power, strength and authority. Although these words may not be familiar to you unless you have studied Greek terminology in the Bible, you have probably seen the moral and ethical power that works through them. *Kratos* and *exousia* are generally seen and accepted in Western cultural contexts. *Dunamis*, however, is the kind of power that often Western culture does not readily accept.

The meaning behind *kratos*—having "the power to rule over everything"—is at least an acceptable premise to people who may not be Christians but who acknowledge that a "supreme being" or "higher power" probably exists. People take for granted, without the actual proof of a personal relationship with the Lord Jesus Christ, that some power "higher" than themselves exists. They assume that this "supreme being" exercises power over things that are familiar in everyday life—things like the order of the planets and stars or the weather and other physical properties of the earth. The belief then that "some power" has the power to keep the physical world around us under control is not an altogether foreign concept in some Westerners' minds.

The traits that characterize *exousia*—"the legal right to rule on another's behalf"—are even easier to see in Western culture. We see examples of it every day in our court system. For example, in custody or guardianship cases, a judge gives someone the legal right to "rule" over the affairs of another. That person can make legally binding decisions on their behalf—such as in the cases of children, minors or people who have severe mental or physical impairments.

But the word *dunamis* is used when referring to the power we receive when the Holy Spirit comes upon us. When that kind of dynamic power comes into our lives and produces visible results, the Western mind can be slow to accept the reality of it.

"Show Me the Power!"

Our Christian mind-set in the West is the result of a Greco-Roman culture. As a result, we are very cerebral, very cognitive and very didactic in the way we approach certain things. You can pack people into a church, an auditorium or an arena in the Western world and give them a reasonable presentation for the gospel, and they will come to faith in Christ.

But in most of the world, that is not true. The rest of the world isn't looking for clever arguments. They are looking for power. It's like the shop-worn line in a recent popular movie, "Show me the money!" In other parts of the world, the statement becomes "Show me the power!"

For example, most Muslims are very spiritually minded. This fact has frustrated Christians who have gone into Islamic nations and tried to reason biblical apologetics with a people who are spiritually minded.

We say, "The Bible is the real book, the real Word of God."

"Well, we have a Bible—it's called the Koran."

"But the Bible is God's Word."

"Prove it."

"Well, you see, the Bible has gone through so much over the years, and if you put it all together, you'll find out..."

"No, no. I mean *prove* it. I don't want to hear your words. Show me."

"Well, Jesus Christ is Lord."

"Well, we have a lord over us. His name is Allah. And our great prophet was Muhammad."

"Yeah, but Jesus is greater than Muhammad."

"Prove it."

"Well, you see, either Jesus was who He claimed to be or He was a liar or a lunatic."

"No, no. That's not what I mean. *Prove* it. We have teachers in our community, and powerful things happen through their lives. We want to know if your power is greater than our power. If it's not, then what kind of God are you serving?"

If you go into most African villages and try to do a Western-style presentation of the gospel, they will challenge it with their holy men or their witch doctors. They will have people among them who can do all kinds of incredible things, and they will want to know, "Is your God greater than our god?"

In most of the world, people want to see the power of God demonstrated before they are going to believe His Word. In the West, our cognitive intellectual approach may make it harder for us to accept the power of God when it is demonstrated in the lives of people we know, but I believe we want to see it in our world, too.

We talk about possessing the truth, but are our lives more powerful, our personalities more magnetic, our love more infectious? Do our lives work any better than those of pagans? Often, the answer is a resounding no.

But our lives can have power. They *can* be filled with God's *dunamis*. Our lives can work—*but only if we submit ourselves to God's mighty hand.*

God used me once to demonstrate His power by giving me a series of prophetic words for a group that once operated as a cultlike, fringe group of Christianity.

At the time the leaders of this group asked me to speak for one of their major conferences, they had recanted their aberrant theologies and had come into the mainstream church. Their transformation had marked the first time in Christian history that a group like that had come into the truth the way they did.

It also was the first time in the fifty years of this particular event that they had invited somebody who wasn't one of their members to speak. There I was, a Charismatic/Pentecostal pastor ordained by the Foursquare church who had no history with this group except some friendships I had made in the last few years, and I was trying to connect with two thousand of their people at the conference to bring them a message from God.

In most of the world, people want to see the power of God demonstrated before they are going to believe His Word.

As I was addressing them, God started giving me prophetic words about their founder. I was hearing the words, "Here are some things I believe about your founder," coming out of my mouth, and then I began to say the things that God was showing me.

It was as if I were standing beside myself in shock, watching myself and thinking, *No, Dale! You can't do this. Don't say these things!* But what I was saying was not unkind. In fact, it was insight for helping them forgive their founder for some of the ways he had led them into aberrant beliefs. The Holy Spirit showed even me some things about his past and some things that he had gone through.

But I still was in a sort of panic, thinking, *Dale, what are you doing? Are you crazy? You don't know this man!*

As I spoke, people began to weep. Afterward some of them came to me and asked, "How did you know all that about our founder? There are very few people who know those things about him. Did somebody tell you those things?"

And I said, "Yes. I said those things by the power of God because He wanted to reach out to you and allow you to express your forgiveness about the past. He wanted to heal you. The Holy Spirit told me those things."

God will prove to others through your life that His hand of power is extended toward them for their healing, forgiveness and transformation. For Him to use you in this way, you must submit yourself fully under His mighty hand.

You Are Not the Same Old Person

The Bible makes it clear that God's hand of power has raised not only Jesus from the dead, but it also has raised us who believe from the dead. He made *us* alive with the same power that He demonstrated in raising Jesus from the dead. Ephesians 2:1 says, "And you He made alive, who were dead in trespasses and sins."

It is the power that raised Jesus from the dead that God uses to cause us to be born again and come into a new life. It is not some secondary or junior source of power that isn't as great as the power with which He raised Jesus—it is the very same power of God.

Think of it. His power is surging through you. He has made you new and continues to renew you day by day. His power has erased your past and made your future as bright as the promises of God. His power is available to you right now—if you surrender yourself to the mighty hand of God.

Wow! Raised by the power of the mighty hand of God unto new life... the past is wiped away, and the future is before you. God made you a new, resurrected follower of Jesus when He extended His mighty hand of power to you.

No wonder the devil quickly comes along and says, "I have to lie to these people. I can't have them knowing who they really are *in Christ.*" He wants you to believe that your past determines your future. But in fact, your past is not a place of residence. It is simply a point of reference.

Coming to fully embrace who you are—in Christ—is a key work of the Spirit of God when He resides in your life. The more you understand whom you have become in Christ, the more it will change your life for God. God will show you who you are in Christ when you are under the mighty hand of God—seeking Him with all your heart and walking humbly with Him.

The devil does not want you to know who you are in Christ. He knows that if you do not believe who the Bible says you are in Christ, then you will think you are the same old powerless person you have always been. You will not believe there has been a change, a transformation in your life. You will not believe that in Christ you have become a new creation. If you cannot believe that, then you have bought the devil's lie, and he has accomplished his purpose of keeping you bound to him.

Also remember, we will always behave according to what we believe. Believe the truth about what God says you are, and you will behave in accordance with that. Believe the lie about who Satan says you are, and you'll behave in accordance with that.

Your past is not a place of residence. It is simply a point of reference.

If you read the entire Book of Ephesians, you will find Paul saying over and over again: "In Christ . . . in Christ Jesus . . . through Christ." Paul repeats it again and again because he is trying to help us all to believe we are not the same old people when we are in Christ. In Christ, we are people who have the power of God within us because we have Christ and His transforming power within us.

God wants you to know you are new in Him, alive to Him and that there is a capacity in you to live for God and to love others. You have a capacity to fight the good fight of faith and to be victorious because of the fact that the power of God now resides in you.

As Jesus came out of the grave, when you accept Him, you too come out of the grave. We were raised, as He was, to live in freedom. He raised us up with Him and made it possible for us to sit with Him, to share in His authority *and* power as we live our lives according to His will.

You Do Not Have to Live Like a Christian Zombie

Jesus proved that He had the power to raise us from the dead when He came to Bethany to raise Lazarus. When He arrived, He told the people at the tomb to open the tomb. Naturally, they objected, saying that the body of Lazarus would already be decomposing and would smell. Yet, they did what He commanded.

There are things in your life that may seem dead... beyond repair... never to be opened again. You may have closed yourself off to the remotest possibility of certain things ever happening in your life. But God is saying to you, "Move that stone out of the way. Open that up again."

"But God," you object, "it's dead."

God is saying to the "Lazarus" in your life, "Come forth!"

Our God has power over death, hell and the grave. We are not serving some second-class deity. God does not come in second—ever. He doesn't "show" or "place" like some Kentucky Derby racehorse. He wins every single time.

I guarantee that you will never hear the following statement: "And in second place, giving it a valiant effort, the Lord God, the *almost* Almighty."

It never happens, does it?

God has the power to raise people from the dead—spiritually and physically. But let's be honest: Some of us do not really believe that any more than those people standing around Lazarus's tomb believed it. But just imagine what they must have felt when they saw Lazarus come walking out of that grave.

"Loose him, and let him go," Jesus told them. "Get those grave clothes off him."

You may still be walking around with your grave clothes on, too. God has brought you forth into new life in Christ, but you are still wearing the spiritual wardrobe of your old life. You are dressed in the wounds of gossip or slander, physical or emotional abuse, the memories of the painful things that life has thrown at you.

It is time for you to let somebody take that stuff off you. God wants to release the perfume of the power of His Holy Spirit upon you. But you are still carrying the stench of death from something that happened to you, perhaps even long ago.

Some of us are like the zombies of George A. Romero's campy 1968 film *Night of the Living Dead,* except we are Christian zombies, the walking Christian dead. Like Romero's zombies, who shuffled around speechless with no sign of life in their eyes, spreading their state of death to other people, we shuffle around looking as if we are alive—sort of—but we have that distant, detached, vacant look about us, too.

The truth is, we have God's power and authority flowing through our lives—we do not have to remain Christian zombies. With our deadened speech or actions, we affect the lives of others who hear us or see us. We live our lives bound up by the baggage—the grave clothes— that weighed us down in the past—before we opened our hearts to Jesus. If you feel this way or know you are this way, then please believe that I am not saying this to belittle you, to hurt you or to condemn you. I am saying it only to illustrate that even though all of us who are Christians have the power of God in us through the Holy Spirit, for some of us, our lives are still being dictated by the pain of our past rather than the hope of our future.

In Romans 6:4, we discover an amazing fact about our Christian life:

> Therefore we were buried with Him through baptism into death, that just as Christ was raised from the dead by the glory of the Father, even so we also should walk in newness of life.

The Greek word in this verse for *life* is *zoe.* It means "to live, to have life." It has to do with God's eternal life, which is not just a life that has to do with duration, but a quality of life that

God wants to give us in Him. We are instructed to walk in renewal *(kainotes)*, to walk in life *(zoe)*. *Zoe* life is available to each believer. Just as Christ passed from death into *zoe* life, so too we can walk in *zoe* life.

You may feel like a zombie. You may still be wrapped up in the emotional or spiritual trauma of your past, and as such you are "the walking wounded." Like Lazarus, it is time for you to come forth from your tomb in Jesus' mighty name. (See John 11:43.) It is time for you to walk in God's *zoe* life.

Jesus had to tell those who were standing around Lazarus when he walked out from his grave, "Loose him and let him go," because he still had his burial garb wrapped around him. And the people unwrapped the grave clothes so Lazarus could go free.

If you are strong in the Lord, when you hear zombie talk, speak zoe talk.

If you are still wrapped in grave clothes, you will need other people to help you shed your burial garb, too. You will have to submit your life to the process, and you will have to be a part of it by seeking out someone whom you can trust and ask them to help you get free of your past—but you, just as I do, will need help from others in order for the process to be completed.

You may still have the grave clothes of gossip attached to you. You have been accused, maligned or slandered by people. People have said cruel things to you or about you. They have wrapped you up in false accusations, but it is time for you to be freed—and you can be—in Jesus' name.

Jesus sees you as someone lovely and wonderful and beautiful. Heaven sees you as a child of God, cleansed.

Maybe you grew up in a home where very unkind and cruel things were said to you, and you are still wearing the grave clothes of those experiences. Inside you carry the reminders of what they said you were—those hurts are locked in your heart, in your emotions. Maybe they hinder you from being able to connect with other people emotionally, relationally and spiritually. It is time to get those grave clothes off and to come forth into life in Jesus' name.

For those of you who are stronger in the power of God, when you hear God's people talking like zombies, start speaking the power of *zoe* to them. When you hear someone say, "I can't make it. I've always been a failure. I just feel dead inside, and I can't see any way out of my problems," tell them, "Jesus said, 'I am the *anastasis* and the *zoe*—the 'resurrection' and the 'life.' Jesus can call you out of that despair with the same power that He used to call Lazarus out of his grave. He can restore you to life and show you that His life is all that counts for you and is worth living. Jesus has the power to give you hope when you feel hopeless. Jesus will give you His *power* when you feel so much like a failure that you want to die."

Again, if you are strong in the Lord, when you hear zombie talk, speak *zoe* talk. It could be just the life-giving words that will show someone else there is a way out their "grave." You may enable them to believe that the power of God through the Lord Jesus Christ can give them *new* life—*anastasis* and *zoe.*

Say to them, "Let me get those grave clothes off you. You are not a Christian zombie. You are not the walking Christian dead. You are a *resurrected* child of God. God has raised you up out of purposeless, lifeless living into something that is infinitely dynamic because He is infinitely dynamic."

You Serve a Living God

Those of us who serve God do not serve a lifeless system of beliefs or rules that cannot change our lives. We do not serve a lifeless figure from history who claimed to change lives by the power of God but who has no real power today to work good or defeat evil in our lives.

No, we serve the Creator God, maker of the heavens and the earth and everything in them, to whom *all* power belongs.

So why are we afraid? Of what are we afraid? Are we afraid

of our boss, our job, people with whom we work? Are we afraid of debt, afraid that we won't be able to pay our mortgage, our credit-card payments, our school loan, our car payment? Do we fear financial ruin? Are we afraid of our culture, our society—the violence, the impulsiveness, the apathy with which human lives are taken? Are we afraid of our own future, past or present?

No matter what it may be that we fear, we need a jolt of the Holy Spirit, something that will awaken us to the fact that God's power is ours—whether we are male or female, young or old, rich or poor, university educated or just getting out of kindergarten.

This is something my mom understands. She *knows* that the power of God belongs to her.

My mom hates the devil. She has a black belt in Holy Spirit kung-fu fighting. She will say something like, "OK, devil, I've come to defeat you in the name of the Father, Son and Holy Spirit!"

She just goes for it and says in this low, rumbling voice, "Devil, take your hands off my kids. Loose them in the name of Jesus. You can't have them. They belong to God." And when Mom says the word *loose,* she goes, "*Loooose* them in the name of Jesus!" in a way that lets the devil knows she really means it.

I grew up around that. I remember when I was seven years old, my mom was sick and asked me, "Honey, would you pray for me?" I wasn't very spiritually ferocious at age seven, but I did what I was taught.

"Devil," I said, "God's Word says Jesus was wounded for our transgressions, He was bruised for our iniquities, the chastisement of our peace was upon Him, and by His stripes we're healed. I speak to sickness in the name of Jesus over my mom and command it to go now."

And guess what? It left her!

I lived in an atmosphere of high faith for healing. That is my commitment today; that is my belief—that God has mighty power that He worked in Christ "when He raised Him from the dead and seated Him at His right hand in the heavenly places, far above all principality"—not just a little higher, but far above, infinitely higher than the devil (Eph. 1:20–21).

You Are Who God Says You Are

We need to do a little more tough talking about who we really are in Christ. We need more and more to become people who say what the Word says about us. We need more and more to become people who encourage one another with these truths. Our attitude ought to be, "If the Bible doesn't say that about me, then I won't say it about me either."

I am not a triumphalist in the sense that I think we never go through trials, tribulation and trouble. I certainly would not say to you every time you get sick, "Where's your faith?" I would not say to you every time you go through sorrow, "Come on! Stand up like a man!" (Besides, you might say to me, "I'm a woman. Please don't tell me to stand up like a man!")

The fact is, we go through difficult things in our lives, don't we? But the power of God is able to rescue us out of *every* tribulation, out of *every* trouble, out of *every* season of difficulty. As Psalm 34:19 says, "Many are the afflictions of the righteous, but the Lord delivers him out of them all." Sometimes His power comes to us miraculously—in a moment—and sometimes it is the sustaining strength of God that enables us to move a step at a time through challenging seasons.

Sickness can present us with great challenges. Thank God that He sends us, as He did the disciples, to heal the sick. He calls us to proclaim the gospel of the kingdom, but that declaration must be followed by demonstration—because declaration without demonstration is only half the gospel.

Declaration says, "God is all powerful. God can save you."

Demonstration says, "And just so you know that the Word has power, here it is."

That's what happened when Jesus said to Peter, "Let's have a little Bible study."

Peter said, "Sure, that will be fine," and he opened up his home in Capernaum, and people packed the place out. They were eating all his food, moving his furniture around, no telling what else. In Mark 2:1–12 we see that four friends brought their paralyzed friend to Peter's house while Jesus was teaching.

We need to do a little more tough talking about who we really are in Christ.

We have no indication whether or not this man even wanted to be prayed for. I am inclined to believe that he did not want to go. I am inclined to believe he had had it with all of the charlatans and fake faith healers who never did him any good.

The reason I think that is because the Bible says, "Jesus saw *their* faith" (v. 5, emphasis added). He saw the faith of the four friends, not the faith of the man on the stretcher. He saw four men who believed in Him enough to literally break into a house that was overflowing with people so that they could get their paralyzed friend in front of Jesus.

The house was packed when the four friends arrive. I can even imagine the paralytic on his stretcher saying, "You know what, guys? Let's just go home. I never really wanted to do this in the first place. Nothing is going to happen here. Let's go home."

And they are probably saying, "No, we're not going home. We just need an alternate plan."

Suddenly, one of them says, "Hey! Get a rope."

"Wait a minute," the paralytic might have said. "What are you guys thinking? No, no!"

"Get some rope."

"What are you doing?"

"I've got a plan."

"Oh, no. Not another plan."

In the homes built in those days, stairways led up to the

rooftop. Roofs were used as a place to gather, a deck, patio or porch would be used in our society. So these guys took their friend on his stretcher up to the top of the roof.

Then they started tearing Peter's roof off! By this time I am sure Peter was walking around muttering, "OK, this thing has really gotten out of hand. They've eaten all my food; they're spilling it on my rugs and cushions. What else is going to happen?"

Suddenly pieces of the roof start raining down on Peter and others in the room.

"*Hey!* What are you doing up there?"

The four men wanted to get their friend to Jesus so badly that they tied a rope to the stretcher and began to lower the man down into the house from the hole they had made in the roof. Maybe the paralytic was saying, "Guys, please don't do this! You could drop me."

"What are you worried about? You're a paralytic. You wouldn't feel a thing if we dropped you anyway!"

So they lower him down in front of Jesus. Jesus made a remarkable comment to him. He said, "Your sins are forgiven you."

The religious leaders present responded instantly by saying, "What? No one has power to forgive sins but God! This man says He has the power to forgive sins."

Jesus replied to them, "Let me ask you something: Which is easier to say, 'Your sins are forgiven you,' or 'Take up your bed and walk'?"

By this time there was a hush over the house.

"Which is easier to say?"

The religious leaders were silenced. Then Jesus continued by answering His own question. "*So that you may know* that the Son of man has the power to forgive sins, take up your bed and walk!" he instructed the paralytic. Immediately life flowed though those useless limbs and lifted the man to his feet. Suddenly he was walking.

Jesus said to him, "Take up your bed. Go home; you're healed."

"So *that you may know,*" Jesus said.

He was saying it then, and He is saying it today: "*So that you may know* that what I'm saying has life to it, let the sick come, and let's begin to pray for them and let them get healed, in Jesus' name. *So that you may know* that there is power in the Holy Spirit, if you've not been baptized with the Holy Spirit, come and get filled with the power of God. *So that you may know* that the words that we are declaring are true, let the demon possessed and oppressed come and be delivered by the dynamic power of God. *So that you may know.*"

It is not enough for us to make a declaration. There has to be a demonstration.

Maybe you are saying, "That's kind of scary to me."

But the wonderful thing is, when you live your life submitted under God's mighty hand it opens the door for Jesus to fill your life with His authority and power, and the fear just gets thrust out of you in the process.

It is just us, normal people like us or like the twelve disciples, about whom God says, "I want to give you declaration and demonstration unto domination over the enemy."

He wants us to have a declaration of the gospel of the kingdom, a demonstration of the power of the kingdom and a domination over the enemy of the kingdom. Jesus, in effect, has said, "Get going, I'm with you!"

You Can Live in Peace Because of His Power

In Matthew 6:25, Jesus says, "Therefore I say to you, do not worry."

The Lord Jesus Christ is saying to you, "Do not worry. Stop worrying."

This reminds me of a child who is frightened of a thunderstorm, but finds comfort in the arms of his father. While the earthly father cannot change the thunderstorm one bit, our heavenly Father controls everything—and in the shadow of the Most High, we are truly in a place of no worries.

It is not enough for us to make a declaration. There has to be a demonstration.

"Well, God doesn't really mean *don't worry,*" you might be saying. "He probably means don't sweat the big stuff—you know, don't stress out about whether or not I'm saved, whether or not I have eternal life. He's saying don't worry about stuff like that.

"But He can't be telling me not to *worry*. I mean, if I have a flat tire at night, and I'm by myself and a stranger pulls over to see what's going on, I'm probably going to worry. Everybody *worries.*"

Well, let's see if your theory is correct.

"Therefore, I say to you, do not worry about your life," He says (v. 25).

That seems pretty comprehensive to me.

Jesus continues, "Do not worry about what you will eat or what you will drink, nor about your body, about what you will put on" (v. 31, paraphrased).

> Is not life more than food and the body more than clothing? Look at the birds in the air, for they neither sow nor reap nor gather into barns; yet your heavenly Father feeds them. Are you not of more value than they? Which of you by worrying can add one cubic to his stature?
>
> —Matthew 6:25–27

Well, not me. That's one of the things that I actually worried about at one time. When I was in high school, I wanted to be taller. My sport was basketball, and I had dreams of playing big-time college basketball.

"Am I ever going to grow?" I would fret.

And finally the word came out of heaven, "No, you're not."

Today I am all of five feet eight inches tall. I worried about my stature, but all that worrying did not make me grow one inch. Ultimately it accomplished absolutely nothing.

"Consider the lilies of the field, how they grow. They neither toil nor spin," Jesus asks in verse 28.

You know what He's saying? He is stating the very obvious to show us how pointless our fretting is. You will never find "grunting" lilies. They do not toil; they do not strive hard at it, and they do not spin in distress. You will never find any lily bulbs underground, stressing: "Is it really going to happen? When spring gets here are we really going to grow? Is it really going to happen?" Flower bulbs simply do not worry about such things.

This is the way the Christian life should be. It is supposed to work. Instead of worrying, we need to get under the mighty hand of God and start living out the power and authority He has already given us and expects us to use.

"Therefore, do not worry, because your heavenly Father knows that you need all these things," Jesus was saying. "Just seek first the kingdom of God and His righteousness, and all these things will be added to you" (vv. 28–33, paraphrased).

And as if He hasn't made His point clear enough to them, Jesus adds, "Don't even worry about tomorrow because tomorrow will worry about its own things" (paraphrased).

Think about it this way: Every time the holiday season rolls around, you may start worrying. You worry about Thanksgiving. You worry about Christmas.

"I don't know what we're going to do this year!" you say. "I've got to take care of this, I've got to take care of that. I've got this to do, then there's this and this and this and..."

Stop! Stop worrying! God's hand of power will give you power over distress if you turn over your cares to Him. Be at peace. God has it covered. God will lead you and guide you.

"But you don't understand, Dale. I'm the designated worrier for our family. It's my family job. I inherited it from my mother. She passed it on to me, and her mother passed it on to her. You probably wouldn't understand, but I'm the official worrier."

Actually, I do understand. I understand that your worrying is not helping anyone. You are not making your family times any happier by worrying. The others might be glad, instead, that family times are over just so you will be quiet. Your running around like a crazy person does not make others happy.

In 2 Timothy 1:7 Paul tells Timothy, "God has not given us ... fear ... but power."

You *do not* have to fear the future. Jeremiah 29:11 says God has plans for your future.

You *do not* have to fear failure. Philippians 2:12–13 says it is God who is in you working both to will and to do His good pleasure. Remember, God is *in* you working *for* you.

Let me say that one more time: *God is in you working for you.* Start believing that and accepting it.

Some of us believe more in our local TV news channel than we believe in Jesus Christ: "Channel 5—Working for *you.*"

And we all go, "Yes, yes, I believe it."

We do not doubt that the news team is out there getting the news. We do not even question it. We do not doubt that the local anchors and field reporters are doing their work so that when you and I turn on the news we have the latest stories, whether they are important or not.

Can you imagine what you would think if in the evening you turned on your television, and all the broadcasters were just sitting around clueless about what was going on in your city?

"Well, I really don't have anything for you tonight," the lead anchor deadpans into the camera. "Some stuff came up, and I had a lot of laundry to do. I just never got around to the news."

"Don't have a clue on the forecast," the weather guy pipes in. "There's some kind of front moving over here, and a few things are happening over there. Could be rain, could be snow, could be sleet, could be a tornado, could be a beautiful day, but I have no idea. So just in case, lay out a sweater, a tank top *and* a bathing suit—just get it all ready. Then you'll be ready for whatever happens. Now on to sports."

"Never caught a game today, folks. Sorry," the sportscaster adds. "The arena football team might have won, might have lost, or they might have tied. I have no idea. The baseball game? Never got around to watching it. I got sidetracked."

Let me tell you that the switchboards at Channel 5 would be lighting up *fast.* Because when Channel 5 says, "Working for *you,*" we all believe it. We do not even question it.

So why do we find it so easy to question God when He says in His Word that He is in us working to will and to do for His good pleasure?

Psalm 80:17 says:

> Let Your hand be upon the man of Your right hand, upon the son of man whom You made strong for Yourself. Then we will not turn back from You; revive us, and we will call upon Your name. Restore us, O Lord God of hosts; cause Your face to shine, and we shall be saved!

The psalmist is saying that when the mighty hand of God comes on you, you have the power *to not turn back.* You have the power to be revived—God will bring life back into you even in the most difficult circumstances. You have the power to be restored—God will restore you to Himself because He is in the restoration business. He restores our lives from sin, bondage and a powerless existence and makes something glorious out of our lives so others will see what He is able to do for them.

Make up your mind, because God is for you. Bring every area of worry and weakness under the mighty hand of God's power.

We Look to You, Jesus

In these days of fresh surrender,
We have bowed before Your throne.
We have sensed Your love so tender;
Your refreshing we have known.
Yet we sense there's something coming
Greater than we've known before.
We're so grateful for Your goodness,
Still, our hearts cry out for more.

We look to You, Jesus;
Revive us, our King.
Come show us Your glory;
Come do a new thing.
We look to You, Jesus,
Your will, our desire.
Lord, send forth Your power
And fill us with Your fire.

We have heard Your call from heaven,
Lay aside our weight and sin.
Look away from all distractions,
Run the race by grace within,
For the joy that's set before us,
By Your voice that leads our way,
We will follow to the finish.
We will see You face to face.

—Lyrics by Dale Evrist and Gary Sadler

CHAPTER 12

A HAND OF PURPOSE

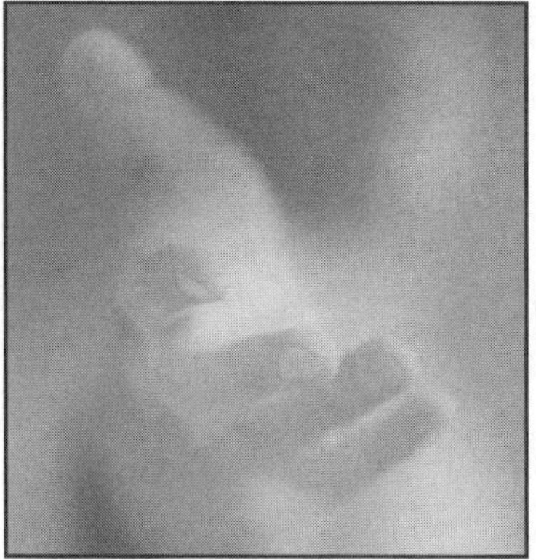

By his mid-eighties, Chuck had served the Lord in some ministry capacity for more than five decades. For most of his life he had enjoyed working passionately for God, had been excited by God's purposes for him and had done what God called him to do. Chuck had always wanted to make an impact for the gospel.

But as he aged, Chuck became housebound due to his age and some physical difficulties, which included an ongoing heart condition as well as some diminished capacities in terms of mobility that can come to anyone as they enter into their latter years of life. One day, rather than going out to lunch or dinner as we had so many times in the past when we spent time together, on this occasion we visited in his home. As I came into his home, his wife, Dortha, told me how pleased Chuck was that I was coming to see him.

"He always perks up when he finds out you're here," she told me, before adding that the recent season in Chuck's life had been a very difficult one for him.

When I walked into the room, Chuck was sitting in a chair, and though his physical capacities were limited, I could sense that the same fire and passion were burning in his heart for God that I had always seen in him.

As I sat down and we exchanged pleasantries, Chuck said to me, "I get so frustrated, Dale. If God wants to take me home, I'm fine with that. But while I'm still here I want to be used for God, and I don't see how I can be."

It was obvious that Chuck was wrestling with a loss of purpose for his life. If God no longer had a purpose for him, then he wanted to leave this life and go to be with the Lord. If God still had something for him to do, then he wanted to stay and know what God's purpose was so that he could do it.

"Chuck, do you still pray for our church every day?" I asked.

Chuck and Dortha had been part of the leadership at the church I pastored in California and had always been very faithful mentors and prayer warriors for Joan and for me, as well as for our church.

"Oh, without fail," he answered.

"Do you still pray for Joan and our family?"

"Yes."

"Do you pray for our denomination every day?"

"Yes."

"Well, then, let me bring you up to date on some of the things that are happening."

His face brightened as I began to tell him what God was doing in our lives, in the lives of the people in our church and in those connected to our church who were either church planters or missionaries. He was excited to hear how his prayers were having a direct effect on all of that.

"So, what you're saying to me, Dale, is that even though all I can do is sit here in the living room of our home and pray, that I'm still having an impact and still helping to change the world?"

"Oh, absolutely," I said to him.

Soon after our visit, I had a plaque made for Chuck and Dortha, and we shot a video of it being presented to them, which we gave to them as well. The inscription on the plaque read: "To Pastor Chuck and Dortha: In honor of making your living room an international house of prayer."

God never closes one door without opening another.

What was especially significant to me at that time was that a number of years before this, Chuck had begun to suffer with some of the heart problems that I mentioned earlier and appeared to be at death's door. In those earlier years he was tempted to give up, and I said to him, "Pastor Chuck, are you done?"

"Am I done? What do you mean, Dale?" he had asked.

"Is your vision for your future here on earth gone? Because if all you can see is heaven, then I'm ready to let you go. You're a man who has lived a full life for Christ, and I'm not ready to keep you here a moment longer than you need to be here. But first I want you to go to God and see if you have any vision left for the future." After he prayed about my words to him, Chuck discovered that he still had a purpose for living.

Chuck later told me with confidence, "I'm not finished yet, Dale."

Then I had encouraged him not to give up in any way but to fight in faith against those things that were afflicting his body. He did that, and now more than a decade later I was honoring him and Dortha with a plaque for their faithful intercession and support in prayer.

Chuck has come to realize that for as long as he is here, God's hand in his life is a hand of purpose. God has shown Chuck that his purpose now, though it is different from his earlier work in leadership at our church, is to reach out from his living room to touch people in intercessory prayer and to fulfill a ministry as a personal intercessor for my wife and me, our family and church. I believe only eternity will reveal how many things Chuck and Dortha have prayed my family and our church through that only God has known about. Chuck's life reveals that God *never* closes one door without opening another.

This will be true for all of us as long as we are serving God with our lives fully submitted to Him—no matter how long we live. The span of God's mighty hand of purpose is big enough to cover your entire life or my entire life. His same hand of purpose that points the way for you today will point the way for you all the days of your life.

God wants each of us to know, just as he wanted Pastor Chuck to know, His purpose for us—where we are to go, what we are to do and how we are to do it.

God Has a Good Plan for Your Life

Do you know that before you were born God knew you? Do you know that God could see your life before He ever embarked on "Day One" of the Genesis creation? He knew back then what He wanted you to be and do today. Now, through our lives being submitted to Jesus, He is able to fulfill His vision of long ago and make us His workmanship.

> For we are His workmanship, created in Christ Jesus for good works, which God prepared beforehand that we should walk in them.
>
> —Ephesians 2:10

You and I are created in Christ Jesus for something marvelous. That's what *good works* means—something marvelous. That means God has a good plan for your life.

When God says we are His workmanship, in the Greek

language He uses a beautiful imagery that is not translated as well into English. The word for *workmanship* in Greek is *poiema*, which means "God's special handiwork, His unique creation, His work of art." It is from the root word *poiema* that we derive our English word *poem* or *song*.

God wants your life to be like a beautiful song or work of poetic verse. God wants to make your life into a masterpiece that tells others a story about Him, a work at which people will look and say, "What has happened in your life is amazing. How did it happen?"

A lot of us, however, feel that the reverse of Ephesians 2:10 is true, as if it really is saying just the opposite about us: "For we His workmanship, created in Christ Jesus *to live lives of despair.* We are His workmanship, created in Christ Jesus *for being nothing but outcasts.* We are His workmanship, created in Christ Jesus *for something that is dull and boring and will go nowhere.*"

That, of course, is not what the Bible says about you or me. God says you and I are His handiwork, His poem, His song. He is writing the lyrics of His life on our hearts and then allowing our lives to become a song to the people around us and to the world. When that happens, we have an open door to talk about the God who calls us with a purpose.

You know, this will deliver you from a faulty image of yourself if you will really believe it. But it requires getting your eyes off yourself and onto who you are in Christ. When you start seeing yourself for who you are in Christ, you will start seeing that you have a God-ordained purpose, and you will stop shelling out dollar after dollar of hard-earned money on whatever new self-help book is out there. When you start meditating on what the Word of God says you are in Christ, you might just realize, "Hey, I *really am* His workmanship, a masterpiece in process."

Which is *exactly* what you are.

Your Life Is Not an Accident

Do you know that when you got saved you did not *sneak* into the body of Christ? Do you know that when you were born again, it was not by a fluke of God-originated power? Do you know that you are not a spiritual accident?

From His throne in heaven, God is not interrogating His angels about you and saying things like, "Hey, how did *he* get in here?" (Or *she*, of course.)

"Well, God, he was at a meeting and somebody gave a call to receive Your Son, Jesus Christ, and he...uh...well..."

"Oh, no! I didn't plan on that. So he really believed?"

"Yes, God, he did."

"Well, I guess I have to save him then, don't I?"

"Well, yes, Father. But what shall we *do* with him?"

"Gosh, I have no idea. I guess I didn't plan on him being part of our family."

That is *not* the way God thinks about you. He is not like a dinner host who had the table set and a meal planned for eight, and then you—the ninth person—showed up unexpectedly, and now He isn't quite sure what to do about you.

Some of us feel that way in our relationship with God, though. We feel as if we are the ones who somehow just slipped in the side door of the kingdom.

He has a specific life plan that He has bestowed on every one of us that He wants to see accomplished—a "Master-planned" life.

And as a result, we think God is telling us, "OK, listen, somehow you got saved. There's nothing I can do about that now. Stuff like this happens to Me, well, because I'm God. Sometimes I'm not looking—I'm busy being so gracious and merciful, and somebody I didn't plan on getting saved gets saved."

"Yes, Father."

"So, now you're going to spend eternity in heaven with Me after you die. I'm afraid you aren't going to be in the *great* part of heaven, but listen, the bargain side of heaven is better than hell. So just be glad you're saved."

"Yes, Father."

"I really don't have a plan for your life because I just didn't plan on your getting saved in the first place. So, there's really *no plan* for your life."

"OK, Father."

"So, hang on the best you can during your pitiful earthly existence, be glad you're saved, and then come and live in heaven when it's all over. OK?"

"Yes, Father."

Most of you know as well as I do how crazy that is. That is *not* the way God is.

But some of us live our lives as if that *isn't* crazy, and we act as if there isn't a plan for our lives. Yet God says He is the master builder and the master planner (Heb. 11:10).

A "Master-Planned" Life

I believe God's hand of purpose will reveal to all of us the master plan that He has for our lives and is working to fulfill for each of us. He has a specific life plan that He has bestowed on every one of us that He wants to see accomplished—a "Master-planned" life.

That simply means God has a preordained plan for your life—and He even has plans for how He will fulfill His plan for your life, and all of those plans are good.

> "For *I know the plans* that I have for you," declares the Lord, "plans for welfare and not for calamity to give you a future and a hope."
>
> —Jeremiah 29:11, nas, emphasis added

"I know the plans I have for you," God says. That means you are not without purpose and destiny in the eyes of God. I know you have probably heard this before—"God has a plan for your life"—and by now you probably think it sounds very much like a cliché, and it certainly can. But whether it sounds like a cliché or not, it is nonetheless absolutely true. We know

it is true by reading what God said to the prophet Jeremiah when He called him for the purpose of prophesying God's will for the nation of Israel:

> Before I formed you in the womb I knew you; before you were born I sanctified you; I ordained you a prophet to the nations.
>
> —JEREMIAH 1:5

Jeremiah's life was not an accident. His purpose was not caused by a happenstance decision on God's part. The Bible makes clear that his calling to do what he did—to be a prophet—was chosen for him and preordained by God.

I believe that God sees your life and mine with that same value, that same sense of purpose, that same desire to call us and bring us into His preordained plan for us. He has for each of us a "Master-planned" life that He wants to accomplish.

And because He does, He does not want you or I to go off course, to get off His track. In order to help keep us on track, in Psalm 32:8 God promises to lead us in His plan:

> I will instruct you and teach you in the way you should go;
> I will guide you with My eye.

God's promise to teach us the way we should go should prevent us from wanting to settle for living someone else's life instead of our own. It would be a tragic thing to never fulfill our own special, God-chosen purpose simply because we were busy fulfilling someone else's expectation or opinion of what we should do.

Yet how many people do that?

How many of us are doing our life's work simply because it is the same thing our fathers or mothers did? There is nothing wrong with following in the career path or the ministry calling of your father or mother—if that is what God is calling *you* to do as well.

I wonder how many men and women there are, for example,

in Bible colleges who are there because their moms and their dads were in the ministry. I have known them myself. I went to school with kids like that. I could see that there was not a call to ministry on their lives, yet they continued to follow a path that had been prepared for their parents but not for them.

But this is also true of any one of us who is doing something that is familiar because it is comfortable or because it is what some person—parent or otherwise—expects of us. It is in the process of doing it that we often discover that it was not what we were created for. For each one of us, what is of utmost importance, if we are going to fulfill the God-given destiny that we have, is to discover God's plan for our lives and then enter into that plan with Him.

Staying on God's Path

I believe with all my heart that if we are going to stay on God's path and find His purpose for our lives, then we are going to have to become broken people before Him. By that I mean we are going to have to absolutely surrender our lives to Him. We cannot play the game any longer of living life as if we are lords instead of disciples.

God has unbelievable plans and purposes for our lives, and He has predetermined a way for us to fulfill them. He has prepared the way for us to walk so it can be fulfilled, and He will point the way for us. But we have to present ourselves to Him and say, "I'm ready to walk in Your way for my life."

If we are going to walk under the mighty hand of God and experience the things God has for us, then there needs to be a commitment in our hearts that says, "I am willing to do whatever You want me to do, Lord." And that commitment needs to hold true during those times when things are tough.

It's when we feel cramped by His narrow path that we are tempted to say, "God, what are You doing with my life? I don't like it. I want to break out of this. I feel confined. Don't You love me anymore? Can't You do anything better with me?"

Sometimes it is the life situation in which He has placed you that makes you question Him and take exception to the path you are on. Whether we ask the question, "What are You doing, Lord?" or turn it into a statement like, "You're not doing right by me, God," what we actually are saying to the Lord is, "I've come under Your mighty hand, and You are not shaping me into the person I want to be. Your way is too narrow for me."

The Bible says it is a tough thing when we begin to strive with our Maker. "Woe to him who strives with his Maker!" (Isa. 45:9). Have you *never* submitted to the shaping work of God in your life? Do you feel that you are *always* in a bad place?

Maybe you have told God, "I am not going to yield to Your shaping work in my life because I don't trust You. I think I have a better idea on how to make me the way I would like to be."

We cannot play the game any longer of living life as if we are lords instead of disciples.

Try saying instead, "Lord, *You* are my Maker. I will not strive with You. I will submit to You, God, and I will submit to the work that You want to do in my life because I believe that You are making a masterpiece, whether or not it looks that way to me or to anyone else right now."

Isaiah 64:8 says:

> But now, O LORD, You are our Father; we are the clay, and You our potter; and all we are the work of Your hand.

When times are tough on us and we are on God's "potter's wheel," He wants us to remember: "Don't forget who I am. I created the heavens and the earth. I created all humanity. I am well able to bring you into the image that I have purposed for you. I am able to direct all your ways so that you will become a person of redemption, so that you will become a person whose life is the story of My glory. I am able to direct you so that I can use your life in My purposes."

The Narrow Way to Life

Your purpose ultimately flows out of your submission to the living God and whatever He has for your life, whatever He wants to do with your life, whatever calling He places on your life.

That truth is a tough sell in cultures where people are taught they can, within the parameters of the law, do whatever they want, whenever they want.

But Jesus said:

> Enter by the narrow gate; for wide is the gate and broad is the way that leads to destruction, and there are many who go in by it. Because narrow is the gate and difficult is the way which leads to life, and there are few who find it.
>
> —Matthew 7:13–14

Jesus said that the kingdom of God lays down some very narrow parameters. The broad way, He said, leads to destruction. Both ways say, "This way to Life," but only the narrow way leads to life.

Not long ago, I was watching a television show about a group of friends who had gone on an exploration adventure in the wilderness of New Mexico. Unintentionally these men wandered off the path they were on and gradually became increasingly disoriented. Having no guide who could find the trail, they eventually ran out of food and water. Then they panicked because they believed they were hopelessly lost.

One of the friends grew so desperate that he begged his friend to kill him. His sense of hopelessness and the pain he was in from starvation and dehydration had driven him to the point that he could not bear to live any longer. Obliging his request, his friend stabbed him to death.

Tragically, they did not know that they were only three hundred feet from the path.

Eventually they were found. During an interview the TV reporter said to one of the survivors, "You were only three hundred feet from a clear path that, if you had followed it, would have taken you out of the wilderness."

"We were so disoriented," he answered, "we couldn't see the path."

Adding to their tragedy was the fact that the one who had stabbed his friend was being charged with murder. It was a calamity that could have been averted if they had only stayed on the path.

It is dangerous to get off the path. That's what Jesus was saying: The path, which is narrow, leads to life. The broad way—all of that expanse that is not part of the path—looks promising and exciting, but in fact, it leads to death.

The Broad Plain of Grace

It is a fact that, for some of us, when the path gets too rough we lose hope. I have heard people say, "I finally got tired of waiting for God. I got tired of waiting, so I did things my way."

At a time like that, if you are not living by prophetic assignment, you will start thinking, *I don't need this. The circumstances are too hard.* At that point you will start to quit on the purposes of God.

But in trying to find our way, God is there with us saying to us, "Don't do it. Don't quit. You've wandered too far this way. Over here—this is the way I've called you to go. Walk in it."

We must believe, though, that in the midst of God's prompting at such a time, He is extending great grace that says, "If you've wandered, just come back."

Even though God's narrow path leads to life, when we are really surrendered to Him, He has a wide expanse of grace around His path that allows us to survive if we make some false moves—because we all are susceptible to wandering.

But if we are really surrendered to the Lord, God is going to lead us and guide us to life. His plans for us are good, and His purposes for us are life-giving.

If you are thinking, *I wish I would have known this twenty years ago*, or if you are thinking, *I really do believe this, and I've tried to live this way all my life and still made a ton of mistakes*, then welcome to the club. It really isn't about *us*. It is about God's *way*. It is the way that works. We just need to stay on it.

We do not need to live in stark terror of a "one-false-move" walk with God—where we will crash and burn if we make one false move, one wrong decision, go in one wrong direction or miss God's will on something. On the other hand, when God is saying, "This is the way; walk in it," and we don't do it, then there are serious ramifications of that choice.

As a pastor I have seen couples give up prematurely on a marriage. Then later they tell me, "Now that I've watched my life, and yours, it's become clear to me that we gave up too soon. If we had just leaned into God and trusted Him more—and leaned into one another—we could have made it."

And I have also witnessed a new spouse say to the former spouse, "I know that he (or she) isn't perfect, but I'm amazed that you let him (or her) go. He's (she's) been an unbelievable blessing in my life."

Even though God's narrow path leads to life, when we are really surrendered to Him, He has a wide expanse of grace around His path.

Experiences like divorce and broken marriages could be so devastating for you that you could be thinking that you would like to quit pursuing God's purpose for your life. You could be so disillusioned or emotionally, spiritually or physically drained that you want to quit trying to fulfill God's will for you.

But resist that temptation to give up. Don't quit on God, because He hasn't quit on you. If you are going to live under the mighty hand of God, then learn not to quit—because God is not a quitter.

If you are upside down in life—if you have made conscious decisions in defiance of God or if you have made decisions in ignorance—or if you have decided that you are not satisfied being the CEO of your life and you are thinking, *I don't like things the way they are, but I don't know what to do about it*, then Psalm 40 is for you.

There is incredible language in this psalm—both metaphor and reality are used—in a theme that says, "He pulled me up."

> I waited patiently for the Lord; and He inclined to me and heard my cry. He also brought me up out of a horrible pit, out of the miry clay, and set my feet upon a rock, and established my steps. He has put a new song in my mouth—praise to our God; many will see it and fear, and will trust in the Lord.
>
> —Psalm 40:1–3

There is a purpose for God's pulling us up. Again, God wants our lives to be the story of His glory. He wants to make us a sign and a wonder: a sign that will make people wonder about Him, about who He is, about what He's like.

If you are going to live under the mighty hand of God, then learn not to quit—because God is not a quitter.

Our lives should be like a sign. A sign always points to something beyond itself. That is its purpose. If we are living under the mighty hand of God fully as we understand it, everything about our lives should have a story attached to it that points to Him. Or as the apostle Paul put it, we get to be a living letter read by all men:

> You are our epistle written in our hearts, known and read by all men; clearly you are an epistle of Christ, ministered by us, written not with ink but by the Spirit of the living God, not on tablets of stone but on tablets of flesh, that is, of the heart.
>
> —2 Corinthians 3:2–3

People read the stories of our lives, and they learn about

God from them. I believe that's because in blessing us, God also wants to bless others through us. He blesses us to make us a blessing—as He did with Abraham.

Let's say that you did not have a good relationship with your dad. You start to talk with someone who does not know God but who understands what it means to have a poor relationship with his or her father. And during your conversation that person asks, "So you didn't have a good relationship with your father? If we're shaped by our environment, then how did you make it?"

"God reparented me," you say.

"God *reparented* you? He does that?"

"Yeah, He does that all the time."

"Then I don't have to live my life as a victim of my environment and my circumstances?"

"No."

"My past doesn't determine my future?"

"No. Your past is a point of reference, not a place of residence. That is where you come from, not where you're going."

Relax, You Are Not Perfect Yet

I am saying, of course, that you and I are not perfect in all that we do. We know and see in part; therefore, we make mistakes. But our goal should be to please God in everything, whether or not we get it right every time.

I'm flawed, too, just as you are. But that is not stopping me. That is not keeping me from believing what God says about me, that I am His workmanship, created in Jesus Christ for good works—for a good purpose—that He preordained that I should "walk in," or live out. I choose to believe God instead of someone else's opinion about me (which, on occasions, includes my own). I also choose to believe Philippians 1:6, which says:

> Being confident of this very thing, that He who has begun a good work in you will complete it until the day of Jesus Christ.

Suppose you were to say to me, "You know, Dale, you have areas in your life you need to grow in."

"I'm guilty. I agree," I would answer.

"You know, Dale, you actually have a long way to go in becoming like Jesus."

"Sure. I agree. Absolutely."

"You know what, Dale? I don't think you're ever going to make it. In fact, you're worthless to God. God's anointing isn't on you, and God has left you. God's not with you at all any more."

"No way. That's a lie," I would say.

It is a lie because God says I am *His* workmanship—not my own. It is a lie because God says the good work that He has begun in me He will complete. I choose to believe what He says about me instead.

That decision is the same for you. You have to choose whether to buy the lie or believe the truth. Remember, the truth, just like the lie, has power only if you believe it.

I could encourage you every day from morning till night with these words: "Hey, God loves you! God has prepared a way for you. You're His workmanship. You're His *poiema*. You're created in Christ Jesus for good works. And as author John Mason has said, 'You were born an original; don't die a copy!' Don't live somebody else's life. Find the incredible plan God has for your life. There are wonderful things He wants to do with you."

I could tell you that all day long every day, but if you are not open to believing it, then it will not help you.

Sometimes I imagine that when God talks with us, to Him it must resemble one of my favorite cartoons from Gary Larson's retired *Far Side* comic strip. It's the one in which a pet owner is trying to get his dog and cat to listen to him and obey him.

"Come here, Sparky! Right now, Sparky! Come here, Sparky!" the man calls.

And what does Sparky the dog hear?

"*Blah-blah-blah*, Sparky! *Blah-blah-blah*, Sparky!"

"Come here, Mittens! Over here, Mittens! Come here, Mittens!" he calls to his cat.

And what does Mittens hear?

"*Blah-blah-blah-blah-blah-blah.*"

Sometimes that's the way we are with God. We are no better at understanding His voice than Sparky and Mittens were at understanding their master. God is preaching His heart out to us, saying, "Listen to Me. You're My workmanship! I've prepared the way for you. I have a plan for you to fulfill, good works for you to walk in! My mighty hand is a hand of purpose for you! Believe Me!"

And what are we hearing?

"*Blah-blah-blah-blah-blah-blah*, Bill!"

"*Blah-blah-blah-blah-blah-blah*, Mary!"

"*Blah-blah-blah-blah-blah-blah*, Tom!"

You have to choose whether to buy the lie or believe the truth. Remember, the truth, just like the lie, has power only if you believe it.

It amazes me that at times I can preach a message telling people that God has incredible plans for their lives—how they are His *poiema*, His handiwork, His work of art; how He has a purpose and a plan for their lives. Yet some of the listeners will come up to me after a service, discouraged and depressed, and share with me that they are not sure God really has a plan for their life. As I listen to them, I think, *Were we in the same room, and were we reading from the same Bible?*

How much better, as most people do, to have someone come up to me and say, "That really encouraged me, Dale. Would you pray for me? When I came in I was feeling pretty low, but I got hold of what you said today. And I have experienced what you preached about today. I do feel like I'm worthless sometimes. Pray for me, because I'm refusing to buy the lie. I'm going to believe the truth that I am God's workmanship and that He does have an incredible plan and purpose for my life."

Don't Hang Out With Your Hangups

Staying on God's track is a lifetime commitment we must make. When we begin to think we know more than God about anything in our lives, it opens the door to trouble. If we do not let God choose in everything, we may begin to think we are wiser than God. We will start thinking we know ourselves better than God knows us, thinking we know what will make us happy, that we know what will fulfill us. Ultimately we may think we know better than God.

Satan always wraps up some truth in his lies.

Satan, our enemy, does not want us to surrender ourselves to the mighty hand of God. He breathes these words in our ears: "If you surrender yourself completely under the mighty hand of God, He will ruin you. He will take away all your fun. He will take away anything wonderful in your life. He will leave you penniless, and He will leave you lonely. He will make you weird—you won't believe how strange you can become if you give your life entirely to the Lord."

He whispers that lie over and over again to countless teenagers who have their "whole lives," so to speak, before them. What better time for Satan to rob a teen of his or her purpose?

Did you ever think when you were a teenager how weird your life might turn out if you gave it to Jesus? I did. I would be sitting in those evangelistic meetings, and somebody would be giving a call for people to come forward. My heart was pounding from the tug of the Holy Spirit. The throb in my chest made it feel as if my shirt were sticking out a mile.

Inside I was practically begging the guy up front, wishing I could just shout, "Stop it!" And the Holy Spirit was saying, "Come on, come on. Give Me your life."

And the enemy was right there too, talking in my ear as fast as he could, saying, "If you give your life completely to the

Lord, you will be the weirdest, most unpopular person in school." And I was thinking, *I don't want to be weird. I don't want to be unpopular. I want kids to like me.*

But he would not let up. "It will just get worse," he would say. "*No one* will want to hang with you if you make that decision."

Satan always wraps up some truth in his lies. You *do* become different. You *do* become strange—but strange to the world, not strange to God. And you find out that what is *strange* to the world is *normal* for God, and what is weird to the world is wonderful with the Lord.

If you are a businessman, the devil might try saying to you, "If you give your business to God, God will drive your business into the ground."

Or he might try a different tact, like: "God will multiply your money, then He'll make you give every penny away to missions, and you'll have nothing. You'll live in a shack, and people will wonder how can you make six figures and have nothing. Moaning, you'll have to tell them, 'It's because I gave my business to God. He takes all of it. I live on canned chili and soda crackers and make a six-figure income because God takes all my money.'"

The devil will tell you all kinds of lies—any kind of lie that you will fall for—to make you believe God does not have a good plan for your life. He will say whatever it takes to get you to believe that God is in heaven just thinking up something to ruin your life. The enemy will try to convince you that God is thinking, *How can I really mess this person's life up? That's what My mighty hand exists to do—to make this person miserable.*

And if you aren't careful, you will start believing those things. Then you will start feeling sorry for yourself and start asking yourself, "Hey, what about *me?* Life is a challenge, and I'm not getting any younger, you know. I'm really not happy. I'm just not happy."

Let's start to believe what God says about us—that from before creation He has prepared our way, that through Jesus

He makes us His workmanship and that He has a good plan for us to walk in.

God's hand of purpose will predetermine the way—and it will be *good*—if we will walk in it. God had predetermined in His mind His redemptive purposes for Jesus—just as He has for you and I. And what God predetermines He is able to accomplish. He will accomplish His purposes through whoever will cooperate with Him. As a result, His kingdom agenda will advance. God will be able to accomplish His purposes for this earth.

We have the opportunity to partner with God and become a part of His eternal redemptive purposes for mankind. Talk about giving your life away for something wonderful! God has predetermined the way. The question is: Are you and I walking in it?

Do and Say What God Is Doing and Saying

When we come to believe that God's mighty hand is a hand of purpose and that He has a plan prepared for us to walk in, we soon realize that we need Him to show us the way. Because He is the one with the plan, we need Him to point the way toward the path in which His purposes for us can be fulfilled.

Isaiah 30:21 says you will hear a voice behind you, saying, "This is *the way*, walk in *it*" (emphasis added). Notice that I emphasized the words *the way* and *it*. That's because God will show you His purpose for your life, and if you are listening, you will hear His voice.

Sometimes you will hear His voice speaking through another person. Sometimes you will hear His voice when you read your Bible. Sometimes you will hear His still, small voice talking to your heart. Sometimes you will hear His voice in your circumstances. Sometimes His voice will be an impression in your heart. Sometimes it will be a dream; sometimes it will be a vision.

However it's communicated, because God wants so much for you to know the purpose for which you were created, He said that you are going to hear His voice. And His voice is going to say, "This is *the way;* walk in *it.*"

The idea that life is just about multiple choices and that as a believer you can do whatever you want to do is a great way for you to continue smacking against that brick wall called "purposeless living." What a terrible way to live! I am not saying you are not saved. And I am not saying that God does not love you. You may even be somewhat content living that way. But God has a better way for you to live.

God's hand of purpose will predetermine the way—and it will be good—if we will walk in it.

Many of us are creatures of habit. We say, "This is what we always do. We always vacation here. This is what we like to do." Now, don't get me wrong. I think traditions that are of God and have life are wonderful. I'm just saying that if our lives revolve around trying to fit into some kind of comfortable lifestyle in which our concerns are all about a place to live, food to eat, vacations we go on and traditions that we enjoy and are used to, we really have significantly missed what God has called us to. Our pursuit is not meant to be comfort. Our pursuit is meant to be purpose.

I want my life to matter for something. I do not want just to fit into my community. If that's your desire, if you just want to be one more person fitting into your cultural context, then you can do that. But I want to help you lift your eyes to see that God is saying, "I will speak to you, and I will say to you, 'This is the way.'"

And when God says, "This is the way," you can be absolutely certain it *is* the way for you.

When God points the way, when His mighty hand points the way for you, it is a way worth traveling. Will it be an easy way? No. Will it be a way that gives you constant comfort? No. Will it be a way that, after you have walked through it, you will say, "Oh, it was so wonderful to walk with God"? Yes. It will never be a path that you regret walking.

LETTING GOD'S PURPOSE GUIDE THE WAY

There are people, even Christians, who, other than the fact that they are born again, live lives that are the work of their own hands. When we make our lives the work of our own hands, what we ultimately are saying is that our God has no hands worthy of fashioning us. Therefore, we have to take the responsibility of our lives on ourselves. Yet all of us are the same in that we have to bow our knees before God if we are ever going to find His purpose for us.

Our pursuit is not meant to be comfort.
Our pursuit is meant to be purpose.

Many of us are like a horse being broken—we kick, we resist the prodding of the Lord, we shake off His hand upon us, we pull against the tug of the Holy Spirit on the reins of our hearts and we act wild, independent and free.

But in the end, if we do not bow the knee and surrender ourselves under the mighty hand of God, we will not find our God-given purpose—ever. We will never find the reason for which we were born, the reason for which God made us.

If you are unwilling to bow in surrender to God, the unfortunate thing is that God will never be able to use you the way He desires. Instead of a broken and yielded servant, all He has to work with is a very inconsistent part-time servant. He will be able to trust you some of the time, but most of the time you will be all over the place. Occasionally, like the wild horse, you will be willing to let Him get near you. But most of the time, you will be running and going your own way.

We all have to bow the knee. God requires it of us all. I have to. We all have to come before the Lord and say to Him, "Lord, I am willing to lie down completely. I am willing to surrender completely. I trust You. You have never done anything to hurt me. You've never done anything to betray me. You've never done anything that would ever lead me to believe Your plans for me were anything other than ultimately for good."

Whatever difficulties, whatever challenges, whatever training, whatever reining-in that God has had to do with us, it is done to give us life. The bridle of God upon our necks is not intended to restrict us to death—it is meant to release us to life. It has been done with a purpose. It is by His mighty hand of purpose that He has done these things with us so that we will find our predetermined purpose in Him.

If we do not bow the knee and surrender ourselves under the mighty hand of God, we will not find our God-given purpose—ever.

Consider what the apostle Paul said—Paul who had learned whom he was supposed to be in Christ through such absolute surrender that he called himself the "prisoner" of Jesus Christ. (See Ephesians 4:1.) That's a humbling title by today's standards, and it was a humbling title in his day, too. Despite giving himself that title, Paul was the one who, in Romans 8:28, said:

> And we know that all things work together for good to those who love God, to those who are the called according to His purpose.

He so believed in God's purpose for him that he said everything would work together for good because he was called according to God's purpose.

God's hand will always be a mighty hand of purpose regardless of whether you and I acknowledge Him, regardless of whether you and I do what He calls us to do. But if we are willing to live in complete surrender to Him, then we will experience His fullness of joy and our sense of eternal worth.

A New Theme for Your Life: Living Under the Mighty Hand of God

For those of us who are willing to come under the mighty hand of God, He will promote us, He will provide for us, He will protect us, He will empower us and He will give us purpose. It will come under no other terms than absolute surrender. He is Lord, and He is God.

By surrendering absolutely to God, and by living under His mighty hand, we can do all things. In Him we have the capacity to live lives of righteousness unto Him. In Him we have worth and value.

Apart from Him we can do nothing. "I am the vine, you are the branches. He who abides in Me, and I in him, bears much fruit; for without Me you can do nothing" (John 15:5). We can never separate ourselves from that abiding relationship in Him if we want to live lives of power and victory. But who would want to? Under His mighty hand our lives surge with life-giving power—both for us and for those to whom we pass it. Under His mighty hands we partner with God to turn this world right-side up for God.

If you feel your heart resonating with the desire and lifelong theme of bowing to Him in total surrender, just kneel before the Father now and say to Him:

> *Father, I am unwilling to live any other gospel than the true gospel. I am unwilling to live a humanistic gospel. I am unwilling to allow myself to say to You, "Here is what I plan to do: I plan to make something of myself by going out and doing what I want to do."*
>
> *Father, I come humbly. I come broken before You, and I say that I need You in every way. I ask You to reveal Your plan for my life that I may follow You in it and fulfill the destiny You have for me.*
>
> *Father, I submit myself under Your mighty hand, Your hand of promotion, provision, protection, power and purpose, and I believe that I will be used by You to accomplish Your plans and advance Your purposes in the earth during my lifetime.*
>
> *Thank You for placing Your mighty hand over me, under me and around me now. In the name of Your Son, Jesus, amen.*